RETHINKING UNDERGRADUATE BUSINESS EDUCATION

Liberal Learning for the Profession

Anne Colby

Thomas Ehrlich

William M. Sullivan

Jonathan R. Dolle

o

Foreword by
Lee S. Shulman

THE CARNEGIE FOUNDATION FOR THE ADVANCEMENT OF TEACHING

JOSSEY-BASS
A Wiley Imprint
www.josseybass.com

Published by Jossey-Bass
A Wiley Imprint
989 Market Street, San Francisco, CA 94103-1741—www.josseybass.com

Readers should be aware that Internet Web sites offered as citations and/or sources for
further information may have changed or disappeared between the time this was written
and when it is read.

Jossey-Bass books and products are available through most bookstores. To contact
Jossey-Bass directly call our Customer Care Department within the U.S. at
800-956-7739, outside the U.S. at 317-572-3986, or fax 317-572-4002.

Jossey-Bass also publishes its books in a variety of electronic formats. Some content that
appears in print may not be available in electronic books.

Library of Congress Cataloging-in-Publication Data
Rethinking undergraduate business education : liberal learning for the
profession / Anne Colby ... [et al.] ; foreword by Lee S. Shulman. – 1st ed.
        p. cm. – (The Carnegie Foundation for the Advancement of Teaching ; 20)
     Includes bibliographical references and index.
   ISBN 978-0-470-88962-6; 9781118038697 (ebk); 9781118038703 (ebk);
9781118038710 (ebk)
   1. Business education.   2. Education, Humanistic.   3. Undergraduates.   I.
Colby, Anne, date
   HF1106.R47 2011
   650.071'1–dc22
                                                                2011005922
Printed in the United States of America
FIRST EDITION
HB Printing   10 9 8 7 6 5 4 3 2 1

The Carnegie Foundation for
the Advancement of Teaching

Founded by Andrew Carnegie in 1905 and chartered in 1906 by an Act of Congress, The Carnegie Foundation for the Advancement of Teaching is an independent policy and research center whose charge is "to do and perform all things necessary to encourage, uphold, and dignify the profession of the teacher and the cause of higher education."

The Foundation is a major national and international center for research and policy studies about teaching. Its mission is to address the hardest problems faced in teaching in public schools, colleges, and universities—that is, how to succeed in the classroom, how best to achieve lasting student learning, and how to assess the impact of teaching on students.

CONTENTS

FOREWORD

IN HIS BOOK *A Modern College and a Modern School,* Abraham Flexner—famous for his pioneering Carnegie Foundation study of medical education—articulated his vision for the modern undergraduate institution. Published in 1923, Flexner argued that there were three kinds of students served by a modern college—future scholars, future professionals, and future businessmen and businesswomen. The first group comprised those few who intended to pursue graduate work as scholars, professors, or teachers in the fields that constituted the college curriculum. Professionals were those who were headed toward one of the learned professions such as medicine, law, engineering, and the like. Finally, those who were preparing for careers in business or commerce, the future merchants of our society, were in the third category. Thus preparation for business careers was identified nearly a century ago as one of the important missions of higher education.

Flexner was confident that education in the liberal arts and sciences was a necessity for a student in any one of those paths. He had, after all, been liberally educated at the Johns Hopkins University and then had returned to his hometown of Louisville, Kentucky, to found and lead a very successful college preparatory school. For the future scholar, the importance of a broad background in the liberal arts was unquestioned in spite of the fact that he or she would ultimately specialize in a particular field from among those arts and sciences. For the future professional, the argument was somewhat more challenging, but one Flexner put forward with clarity and confidence for medicine and the other "learned professions." But what of that third category, the substantial number of college graduates who intend to become members of the business community? Flexner made that argument for liberal learning with equal enthusiasm. He rested much of his case not merely on the general value of the skills, understandings, and values of the liberal arts for the decisions that characterize the world of business. He also asserted that, like all other educated men and women, future members of the business community also shared the responsibility of active citizenship in a democratic society, and preparation for that role was the most important function of liberal education.

At the Carnegie Foundation, we have not previously chosen to study education for business. Instead, we had examined those fields for which formal professional preparation in universities is a requirement for practice. This meant, however, that we had excluded from our work several forms of professional education that large numbers of students elect to study. Indeed, in recent years business has been the single most popular undergraduate major in the country. Moreover, the ordinary citizen interacts with businesswomen and businessmen far more frequently than with members of other professions.

We may seek medical care rarely, engage a lawyer even less often, and interact with a priest, minister, or rabbi on a weekly basis or not at all. But the world of commerce, of buying and selling, of banks and boutiques, of monthly salaries or foreclosed properties, is the sea in which we take our daily swim. And although one can engage in business without formal academic preparation (just as one can bandage a cut without nursing school and read a novel without becoming an English major), universities and colleges take very seriously their claim that they have the competence and responsibility to educate business practitioners. This book explores the grounds for that claim by seeking examples of the special contribution of higher education to the general intellectual and ethical preparation of business majors.

This book represents, in several ways, a convergence and culmination of more than a decade's work at the Carnegie Foundation from the late 1990s to 2010. Several parallel programs of research were conducted during those years, independent from one another in one sense yet closely tied in another. One line was our work on education in the professions for which formal academic preparation is required. The professions that we studied are law, engineering, the clergy, nursing, and medicine. We also conducted parallel studies of teacher education, but not as part of the general and comparative Preparation for the Professions Program. This work was under the general coordination of William Sullivan and Anne Colby.

The second line of work was our studies of how colleges and universities prepare students for lives of civic engagement and political participation in a democratic society. This work was under the general direction of Anne Colby and Tom Ehrlich.

In addition, there were inquiries into challenges of integrated liberal learning for undergraduates. Mary Huber and Pat Hutchings led some of this work in collaboration with the Association of American Colleges and Universities. That line of inquiry was enriched by studies of "shaping the life of the mind for practice" in which William Sullivan and Matthew Rosin led a team exploring the integration of liberal and professional learning for undergraduates (Sullivan & Rosin, 2008).

These several lines of inquiry were elements of a larger examination (which included studies of the PhD across the disciplines) of how the educational process can prepare students "to profess," to lead lives that require the exercise of intellect, skill, and moral intention for the sake of the greater society. Our method in each of these inquiries was to seek "visions of the possible" rather than primarily to offer criticisms of the offerings that were typical for a given field. Doing so involved identifying the consensus among leaders of the field regarding the most significant challenges that the profession was facing and those places where the most ambitious and creative attempts to deal with those challenges were in place or in development. Extended site visits to those institutions were typically complemented by survey research to tap a broader set of programs and perspectives, and small conferences to review and critique emerging work.

Thus, when our scholars ultimately proposed particular strategies of curriculum, teaching methods, field work, or program rearrangements, the teams could point to places that were already engaged with that kind of work rather than speculate about what that sort of innovation might look like, were someone to undertake it. Visions of the possible serve as existence proofs. They demonstrate that certain pedagogical initiatives can, in principle, be undertaken. Whether educators or policy makers are prepared to deploy the resources, the talent, and the will needed to move from examples to a broad shift in practice is another question.

A starting point for this book was asking the question, "What does it mean to think and live like an educated person?" The answer that is communicated early in this book and reappears regularly is that an educated person is capable of three interacting and complementary modes of thought: analytic reasoning, the ability and disposition to take multiple perspectives when confronting a complex decision or judgment, and finding and making connections of personal meaning between what one does and who one intends to become. Thus a good education prepares a student to dig deeply, critically, and analytically when confronted by a problem; to be able to see that same problem analytically from different points of view; and perhaps most important, to develop a sense of self and of personal identity in which these capacities and dispositions are well integrated. Relating the analytic and the multiple perspectives to the search for personal meaning, the elaboration of a sense of self, and the formation of identity appears to be the key. Ultimately, these liberal and professional capacities are not integrated in the way someone puts the pieces of a complex jigsaw puzzle together; they are integrated via the formation of a sense of identity and personal meaning so that these understandings and dispositions cohere.

As I have looked back on the many studies that my colleagues and I pursued during our work at the Carnegie Foundation, there is a consistent theme at that point in each inquiry when we move from description, diagnosis, and analysis to proposals for change and improvement. Again and again, I find that we recommend greater *integration*. It appears that the most common underlying malady besetting undergraduate education and doctoral education, the education of lawyers or of nurses, the preparation of teachers or of business leaders, is the *dis*integrated character of their learning experiences.

It should probably be no surprise that higher education breeds specialization, distinctiveness, and separation. The dominant social forces in universities are centrifugal, spinning the world apart into more discrete parts whose elucidation is the work of separate disciplines, fields, and professions. We recruit faculty members as experts in these areas, promote them because of their contributions to them, and organize both our catalogues and our libraries to correspond to their topography. The dilemma of universities in great measure is that when the educational goal is to teach students to become adept at practical reasoning in the presence of problems of the real world, the very separations that make the growth of knowledge possible make its educational use problematic. Disciplinary specialization is a powerful way to expand knowledge; it is a terrible way to apply it.

The core problem is not specialization and disciplinary investment per se. The problem is that the parts remain separate and distinct with no complementary strategy or incentive to put Humpty Dumpty back together again. I'm reminded of a conversation I had in the Moscow Academy of Pedagogical Sciences in 1980 with a Professor Posner. He observed, "You Americans fail to understand the important distinction between *individualism* and *individuality* as educational values. When a society values individualism, it rewards the development of personal expertise and talent so it can be used for the benefit and competitive advantage of the individual who possesses those attributes. By contrast, when a society values individuality, it too nurtures the development of individual talent and expertise, but rewards and recognition come when those accomplishments are then directed to the benefit of the larger community and not solely for the sake of the individual." In universities, we readily reward the accomplishments of the individual academic entrepreneur but afford much less support to meeting the challenges of bringing those distinctive talents back together collaboratively for the sake of the institution's educational and service efforts.

This book is filled with vivid accounts of teachers, courses, curricula, and student performances that transcend the centrifugal academic inertia in which curricular motion persists in spinning disciplinary concepts and their meanings further apart over time. These examples demonstrate that the problems can be addressed and we can cite powerful instances in all types of institutions. So why don't these kinds of initiatives occur with regularity?

Such integrations require institutional intentionality, not parallel play. The integrations that are advocated can be achieved only when one or more faculty members are prepared to leave the comfort zones of their personal expertise and embark with their students into the messy domains of practice and practical reason. Moreover, they must be actively mixed together, squeezed and kneaded, shaken not stirred. This kind of integration does not occur by merely adding the humanities to a business curriculum as either prerequisite courses or distribution requirements. The reciprocal infusion of liberal learning and professional development is not like fluoridating the water to prevent cavities; liberal learning and business education do not affect one another by proximity. These educational ends will not be achieved by having business majors inhale the secondhand smoke of Plato and Emerson.

The strategic idea at the heart of the proposals for change is what I would describe as *reciprocal integration*. The authors are not just prescribing the value of the liberal arts to ameliorate the ills of business education in particular or professional and civic education more generally. This is a far more radical proposal. They assert that liberal education itself is also in distress, too often taught in isolation and antiseptically removed from the humans and their problems from which it purports to derive and to which it claims relevance. The concept of reciprocal integration argues strongly that the liberal arts must be professionalized, must be framed and taught in the context of practical problems, at least as much as practical learning needs to be enriched, nuanced, and critiqued through the lenses of the ideas and perspectives of the liberal arts. Each of these domains must serve as both crucible and catalyst to animate the educational potential of the other. Therein lies the most important challenge this book confronts in both of the academic domains that it studies. The concept of reciprocal integration demands intentionality and effort from all those who engage in undergraduate education.

This work was conducted by a "dream team" of Carnegie colleagues who joined together in this program of research. The team comprised Anne Colby, a developmental psychologist who has made singular contributions to our understanding of moral development across the life span; Tom Ehrlich, a lawyer who has served as professor, dean, provost, and president in private and public universities, and as a public servant at the national level, and whose liberal education probably owes at least as much to discussions at the Harkness tables of Exeter as to the lecture halls of Harvard; Bill Sullivan, a classically trained philosopher who has been doing as much social science as philosophy for the past twenty-five years; and Jon Dolle, an engineer turned educational philosopher and policy scholar, who joined the project as a graduate student and soon became a full partner (while earning a Stanford PhD). I tend to believe that this kind of interdisciplinary team could be formed "only at Carnegie" but that would be an exaggeration. It certainly was much easier to accomplish in a community of scholarship and policy that did not have to bear the burden of formal departments, academic disciplines, or an accounting of credit hours or even "Carnegie units."

Would that our team could have come up with a simpler resolution than a call for the very sort of reciprocal integration of curriculum, of teaching and learning, and of institutional culture that our universities and colleges seem designed to resist. Alas, no quick fix presented itself. Teaching and learning are not activities for the faint of heart. Radical transformation of teaching and learning requires intelligence, tenacity, and courage. In that sense, the proposals that emerge from this work indeed echo the century of Carnegie work that began with Flexner's studies of medical education. Acting on Mr. Flexner's proposals produced a painful period of institutional dislocation and creative curricular destruction. And those changes eventually needed repair and renovation as well.

Our proposals to "fix" business education are also proposals to repair the deficiencies of general and liberal education even as the importance of such work becomes more apparent to our society and its leaders. Our proposals to repair the education of PhDs, reported in other books, are also critical here because we cannot ignore that doctoral education serves as the "normal school" for training future university and college faculty members, shaping their identities as it molds their habits of mind and their scholarly and teaching skills.

At the end of a dozen years of work, therefore, we present our colleagues in higher education with a daunting challenge. If you wish to make significant changes for the better in any particular domain of instruction—such as education for business—recognize that you must begin to mess with the entire interconnected and marbled enterprise. If nothing begins to unravel as you begin your work, it's likely you have missed the point.

I know I join all who will read this book and ponder its implications for themselves and their institutions in thanking the authors for the rigor of their scholarship, the engaging clarity and stimulation of their accounts, and the inspiring character of their challenges. To read this book seriously does not engender a sense of comfort and satisfaction with the way things are; yet it does provide a thrilling vision of how they might be. And that has been the role of The Carnegie Foundation for the Advancement of Teaching since that day in 1907 when the Foundation's first president, Henry Pritchett, invited a schoolmaster named Abraham Flexner into his office and invited him to conduct a study of medical education.

LEE S. SHULMAN
Stanford, California

For the many Carnegie Foundation colleagues with whom we have worked and from whom we have learned—in incomparable intellectual community, with abundant hilarity and joy—from 1997 to 2010

ACKNOWLEDGMENTS

IN RECOGNITION OF the collaborative nature of the research for and writing of this book, the three senior authors are listed alphabetically. Our coauthor, Jon Dolle, who was a doctoral student at Stanford during the research and writing, was also our full collaborator. The scheme for describing liberal learning in terms of Analytical Thinking, Multiple Framing, the Reflective Exploration of Meaning, and Practical Reasoning, which is introduced in Chapter Four, was developed by William Sullivan in the context of this project, drawing on his earlier work on Practical Reasoning (Sullivan & Rosin, 2008).

The team was assisted by many others, and we gratefully acknowledge the many people who have contributed to the project and the book. We especially want to acknowledge the help and hospitality extended by the administrative leadership, faculty, and students of the colleges and universities that participated in our study.

We are also indebted to the leadership and staff of The Carnegie Foundation for the Advancement of Teaching. President Lee S. Shulman provided ideal conditions for the cross-pollination of fields and ideas from which this project began. We are grateful to his successor, Tony Bryk, and Carnegie Foundation vice president John Ayers for continuing to provide a home for our work.

We wish to thank our reviewers, Sally Blount, Rakesh Khurana, and Jeff Nesteruk. Through their careful reading of the manuscript and constructive suggestions they enabled the authors to produce a much better book than they could otherwise have managed.

Former vice president of the Carnegie Foundation Patricia Hutchings provided incomparable editorial assistance in the preparation of the book. Her contributions made a huge difference in the cogency and readability of the manuscript.

The authors also owe a significant debt to those among their colleagues who took part in the site visits. Through their patient attention and careful observation, Tony Ciccone, Mary Huber, and Cheryl Richardson greatly enriched the authors' understanding of the educational worlds they helped to explore.

We are also grateful to David Brightman, senior editor at Jossey-Bass, for his continuing support and encouragement.

Both the research and the book have been enhanced by the contributions of Jim Sirianni, then a Stanford doctoral student in education and research assistant to the project. Megan Downey and Dania Wright provided essential support that sustained the project and the writing of this book.

Finally, we wish to acknowledge the financial support of those who funded the project: Carnegie Corporation of New York, the Kauffman Foundation, the Skoll Foundation, and the Teagle Foundation. Without their confidence in the project, this book could not have been written.

THE AUTHORS

ANNE COLBY is a senior scholar at The Carnegie Foundation for the Advancement of Teaching and a consulting professor at Stanford University. Prior to joining the Carnegie Foundation in 1997, she was director of the Henry Murray Research Center at Harvard University. She is coauthor or editor of ten books, including *The Measurement of Moral Judgment, Some Do Care: Contemporary Lives of Moral Commitment, Educating Citizens*, and *Educating Lawyers*. A life-span developmental psychologist, Colby holds a BA in psychology from McGill University and a PhD in psychology from Columbia University.

JONATHAN R. DOLLE is an associate partner for Research and Development at The Carnegie Foundation for the Advancement of Teaching. From 2005 to 2010 he worked as a research assistant at the Foundation on the business education and liberal-learning project. He holds degrees in engineering, philosophy, and education policy from the University of Illinois, Urbana-Champaign. In fall 2009 he was a Mirzayan Policy Fellow at the National Academy of Sciences. In 2010 he received his PhD in education from Stanford University and joined the Carnegie Foundation full time.

THOMAS EHRLICH is a visiting professor at the Stanford University School of Education. From 2000 to 2010 he was a senior scholar at The Carnegie Foundation for the Advancement of Teaching. He has previously served as president of Indiana University, provost of the University of Pennsylvania, and dean of Stanford Law School. He was also the first president of the Legal Services Corporation in Washington, DC, and the first director of the International Development Cooperation Agency, reporting to then-president Carter. After his tenure at Indiana University, he was a Distinguished University Scholar at California State University and taught regularly at San Francisco State University. He is author, coauthor, or editor of thirteen books. He is a trustee of Mills College and has been a trustee of the University of Pennsylvania and Bennett College.

He is a graduate of Harvard College and Harvard Law School and holds five honorary degrees.

WILLIAM M. SULLIVAN is a senior scholar at the Center of Inquiry in the Liberal Arts at Wabash College in Crawfordsville, Indiana. He was formerly a senior scholar at The Carnegie Foundation for the Advancement of Teaching where he codirected the Preparation for the Professions Program. He is the author or coauthor of six books, including *Educating Lawyers*, *Work and Integrity*, *A New Agenda for Higher Education*, and *Habits of the Heart: Individualism and Commitment in American Life*. Prior to working at the Carnegie Foundation, Sullivan was professor of philosophy at LaSalle University. He holds a PhD in philosophy from Fordham University.

LIBERAL LEARNING FOR BUSINESS EDUCATION

AN INTEGRATIVE VISION

BUSINESS HAS NEVER MATTERED MORE. Most people now realize that the livelihood of citizens of Minneapolis is related in complicated ways to the skills and aspirations of the citizens of Guangzhou, Sao Paolo, and Mumbai as well as those of Mobile. The enormous economic expansion within some of the most populous nations of the world, especially China, Brazil, and India, has put competitive pressure on growing numbers of U.S. workers and firms, who compete with others in distant places, even as they also sometimes cooperate through complex networks of trade and investment.

Increasingly, this fragile interdependence is being managed by international business and, over the past several decades especially, by banking and financial sectors that have become tightly linked on a global scale. The "commanding heights" of the economic welfare of nations are no longer occupied by governments alone (Yergin & Stanislaw, 1998). Business in its multiple manifestations has become a prodigious governing force, shaping the destiny of people everywhere.

Business is also more important than ever in American higher education. In 2006–07, the most recent academic year for which national data were available, 21 percent of all undergraduates were business majors. This makes business the most popular field of undergraduate study. When business is combined with other vocational majors such as engineering, nursing, education, agriculture, security studies, and others, the total rises to 68 percent of all undergraduates (National Center for Educational Statistics, 2009).

1

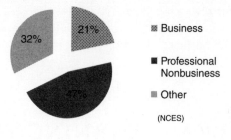

At the same time, the prominence of business institutions in contemporary U.S. society has enhanced the prestige and authority of successful leaders in business, and business ways of thinking have now taken hold in wider sectors, including not only government but also the organization and leadership of the academy.

For higher education, these developments pose an important question. The American academy has been chartered for important public purposes, chiefly to educate citizens for democracy. The centrality of business in society, the great number of undergraduates who choose business as their field of study, and the even greater numbers who will be employed in business for their working lives demand that higher education do more than just help students acquire tools for advancing their personal careers in business, although that is an important goal. In order to ensure that its graduates develop the breadth of outlook and conceptual agility for living in a global century, higher education also needs to ensure that students understand the relation of business to the larger world and can act on that understanding as business professionals and as citizens. The question, then, is how best to do this? What should undergraduate business education provide for students?

The Bell Project

The answers proposed in this book reflect our work in the Business, Entrepreneurship, and Liberal Learning (BELL) project, an initiative of The Carnegie Foundation for the Advancement of Teaching. Simply put, we believe that undergraduate students who major in business should have the benefits of a strong liberal education. Business and liberal learning must be woven together to prepare students for their professional roles and work and also to prepare them for lives of social contribution and personal fulfillment. In this sense, we propose an integrative vision.

Accordingly, our research has focused on how liberal education interacts with business preparation in undergraduate programs, asking how well undergraduate business education has been able to take advantage of the contributions of liberal learning. We began our research with an understanding, which was subsequently reinforced by our observations, that business majors typically experience the liberal arts and sciences in ways that are weak or episodic. Many business students see liberal arts courses as largely irrelevant to their education. For all the reasons discussed previously—and elaborated in the pages that follow—we believe this is unsatisfactory. Therefore, we set out to examine programs that explicitly announced the intent to provide their undergraduate business majors with the benefits of liberal learning, looking both at common principles and concepts shaping their efforts and at the diverse strategies they have employed. These institutions' efforts hold lessons for one another and for the larger field of business education, and we believe they also provide an opportunity for liberal arts disciplines to learn from business education, especially about strategies that help students practice and refine their knowledge in real-world circumstances (see, for instance, Shulman, 1997). Additionally, successful efforts at integration within business programs may be instructive for other professional and vocational programs that wish to do the same.

In this sense, we view business education as an instance of the larger phenomenon of vocational majors, fields of study that aim to prepare students directly for entry into the workforce. Due to the rising costs of higher education and the challenges of the employment market, students and their parents today consider preparation for work a top priority among the goals of higher education, and this preference is reflected in the large percentage of students choosing to major in professional or vocational fields. Because more undergraduate students major in business than in any other single field, it would seem there might be a distinctive character or identity to studying business at the college level. But we did not find this to be the case. Undergraduate business seems to be widely understood as a kind of simplified MBA program. In institutions that offer both MBA and undergraduate business degrees, the undergraduate program rarely has its own faculty or dean and its curriculum resembles that of the graduate program. A more distinctive identity for undergraduate business programs would acknowledge that this is their students' college education as well as professional preparation. This means, in the American tradition of liberal education, that students need to be prepared for their futures as citizens and persons as well as entrants into the workforce.

Rethinking Undergraduate Business Education

To meet the needs of today's increasingly complex context, undergraduate business programs should help their students develop intellectual perspectives that enable them to understand the role of the field within the larger social world. In keeping with this aim, business programs should uphold and cultivate among students a sense of professionalism grounded in loyalty to the mission of business to enhance public prosperity and well-being. To accomplish this, business education must be integrated with liberal learning.

We believe that undergraduate education of every kind should enable students to make sense of the world and their place in it, preparing them to use knowledge and skills as means toward responsible engagement with the world. In order to contribute to the larger life of society, students must be able to draw on varied bodies of knowledge. They need to gain fluency in looking at issues from multiple points of view, which requires the opportunity to explore with others different ways of posing problems and defining purposes. These are the traits that have historically defined a liberal education. In this sense, the question of what business education should provide for students is part of the more fundamental question of what a *college* education should provide.

Research on educational attainment provides abundant evidence that a college education produces significant lifelong effects. College is a prime moment for students, including many older students, to question and redefine their core sense of who they are. It offers the opportunity to expand their understanding of the world and to develop skills they will need to make their way in it. College education enables students to grow as whole persons as well as develop their minds and strengthen their working skills. It helps awaken their intellectual curiosity and self-reflection and can aid their evolution toward attaining a sense of responsibility for the common good.

Today's educational challenge is to prepare students for a world in which ensuring the welfare of the human population must take place within a concern for planetary survival. In such a context, a college education needs more than ever to enable students to understand the world and find their place in it. Beyond that, higher education's mission requires helping students develop so they can and will contribute to the life of their times. These are ideals long espoused by the tradition of liberal education and represented in the core commitments that define professional preparation. These aims have become especially important in the education of business undergraduates today because of the critical and pervasive role of business in contemporary life.

Narrowed Perspectives and Missed Connections

Business programs, like all forms of professional preparation, immerse students in the values and mind-sets that are peculiar to the field; in business this means, most prominently, the logic of the marketplace. This immersion holds the attendant danger that students will lose sight of the larger pluralism of institutional sectors and spheres of value within which business has to operate. This is not just a theoretical concern. Indeed, we found it distressingly common, even in high-quality programs, to hear students say that their business courses had taught them that "everything is business"—overlooking the different values represented by their families, religious congregations, and communities.

Like all undergraduates, business students need the ability to grasp the pluralism in ways of thinking and acting that is so salient a characteristic of the contemporary world. And it is especially important that business students learn to recognize and distinguish between the dominant logic of business and the marketplace, on the one hand, and, on the other, the very different values and ways of acting that hold sway in the family and the domestic sphere, the worlds of science and education, the arts, and within a democratic government. Business graduates will need facility in moving among these different spheres of value and logics of action. They will benefit from learning to see business and its logic from the outside as well as from within.

The need to grasp this pluralism of values and contexts is, we believe, a weak link in the current organization of undergraduate business programs. Most business programs require their students to take a substantial number of courses outside the business disciplines, in classic arts and sciences fields such as English composition, literature, history, the social sciences, science, and mathematics. However, the relation of these studies to students' major courses in business is rarely well articulated or closely coordinated. The overall program as it stands now might be thought of as a curricular barbell: each end of the bar carries a significant weight of intellectual subject matter but the connection is slender. On the two ends of the barbell, students encounter courses taught by different groups of faculty, often from different schools or colleges, who have little contact with their colleagues on the other side of the curriculum. The linkages between the two ends of the barbell receive little explicit attention either in the way the curriculum is organized or in how courses are taught.

This arrangement is not the best way to support the high-quality, interconnected learning that today's students need in order to understand the relation of business to the larger world. In recent decades, research on human learning has made it clear that effective learning depends significantly on learners' intentions and motivation. With business students' focus on career preparation as the most important outcome of college, the goals of liberal education are more achievable if they are explicitly related to students' existing horizon of interest.

Liberal learning has the potential to broaden and reshape such initially narrow purposes but for this to occur students must come to see how and why the perspectives of the arts and sciences disciplines open up and provide insight into matters of concern to them. This requires a kind of teaching that systematically leads students to grasp and participate in making such connections (Kuh, 2008; National Research Council, 2000; Pascarella & Terenzini, 2005).

An Integrative Vision

Our aim in this book is to stimulate and contribute to a national discussion about business education and its future by focusing on approaches that work to integrate the two ends of the usual barbell curriculum. Rather than a barbell, we envision something more like a double helix. Borrowing from the famous DNA model developed by Watson and Crick, we propose the double helix as a metaphor for an undergraduate business curriculum that explicitly and continually links students' learning of business to their use of various arts and sciences disciplines that provide a larger, complementary view of the world.

This is not simply an imagined possibility. As we will illustrate in the chapters that follow, we observed courses and entire programs that explicitly put the disciplinary insights and tools of the social sciences and humanities to use in this way. We first encountered the double helix metaphor at Santa Clara University. There, and in similar programs, we saw the liberal arts and sciences used to provide an understanding of the other institutional sectors that business depends on, such as effective public education systems organized by governments, and the ways in which business affects those other institutional contexts. Through these double helix approaches, faculty as well as students can develop facility in navigating the pluralism of values and operating logics that will mark their graduates' actual lives as business professionals and as citizens.

In the absence of this kind of integrative consciousness, undergraduate business education is often narrow. By this we mean that it provides too little depth of understanding about or flexibility of perspective on the tools and concepts employed in business disciplines. This leads students to view these conceptual tools not as hypotheses to be employed for specific purposes but as simple and complete descriptions of reality. As we will try to show, this limits students' development as thinkers. And, in doing so, it threatens to undermine the creative thinking that feeds innovation.

By contrast, when there is more intentional integration of liberal learning approaches with business—double helix style—faculty can help students achieve more advanced educational goals. They can also strengthen students' sense of professional purpose by showing more effectively how business is interconnected with other dimensions of society and the environment. Implementing this integrative approach will require significant and sometimes difficult reform—that is the nature of innovation. But there is much to build on, historically and in current campus practice.

The Design of the Study

We began our study by surveying business programs broadly, by reading widely in the history of the field and in current business education literature, and by talking with those who have special expertise and experience to share. We also brought to our work a set of ideas and frameworks from Carnegie's earlier studies of preparation in nursing, medicine, the clergy, engineering, and law (Benner, Sutphen, Leonard, & Day, 2009; Cooke, Irby, & O'Brien, 2010; Foster, Dahill, Golemon, & Tolentino, 2006; Sheppard, Macatangay, Colby, & Sullivan, 2009; Sullivan, Colby, Wegner, Bond, & Shulman, 2007).

With a broad sense of the field in view, we chose ten campuses for intensive site visits during the academic years 2007–08 and 2008–09. Our first criterion was to look for places that were committed to bringing liberal learning and business perspectives together in an intentionally integrated curriculum with appropriate pedagogies.

To ensure that we grasped the broad range of issues involved, we also wanted to be sure we visited a variety of program types. We went to several large university business schools. One of these was the Kelley School of Business at Indiana University (IU), as well as the Liberal Arts and Management Program housed in the IU College of Arts and Sciences. Three private university business schools figured in our rounds: the Wharton School of the University of Pennsylvania and the Stern School of New York University along with the Program in Management Science at Massachusetts Institute of Technology's Sloan School of Management. We visited Babson College and Bentley University, institutions begun as business colleges that have evolved into full four-year institutions, as well as Morehouse College and Franklin & Marshall College among predominately liberal arts institutions. Our sites also included Santa Clara University, a Jesuit institution in California, and Portland State University, a public, urban university in Oregon (see "Site Visit Institutions").

Site Visit Institutions

Babson College

Bentley University

Franklin & Marshall College

Indiana University, Bloomington (Kelley)

Massachusetts Institute of Technology (Sloan)

Morehouse College

New York University (Stern)

Portland State University

Santa Clara University (Leavey)

University of Pennsylvania (Wharton)

Our campus visits lasted several days. During that time, we spoke with a variety of academic personnel and students. We talked with deans, faculty, and students in the business programs and the arts and sciences. We visited classes in the business disciplines and the arts and sciences courses frequented by business students, giving special attention to those educational experiences that brought the two areas of the curriculum together. We sought to understand the varying practices of teaching and learning employed in these areas of the business students' curriculum, the kinds of intellectual and social skills that each emphasizes, how students are assessed, and the kinds of moral meaning and professional identity that faculty intend to convey and that students perceive as salient. We interviewed arts and sciences and business faculty individually and held focus groups with students from business and the arts and sciences.

Our aim in these conversations was to understand the experience of business education for faculty and for students and how that is enriched or modified by experiences with liberal learning methods and content. To round out our picture, we also inquired into cocurricular activities and the overall campus climate. We spoke with student affairs personnel and student advisors as well as recent graduates of several of the programs we visited. From these conversations, we assembled detailed pictures of how specific practices of business education focus students' understanding and sensibility and the ways in which integration with the perspectives of the liberal arts and sciences expands and enriches such understanding and opens possibilities for students. These observations and conversations form the basis of the argument this book sets out in the following chapters.

Overview of the Book

Building on the themes and rationale articulated in these opening pages, Chapter Two sets our study and recommendations in a longer-term context. Toward this end, we review a century of developments in which business education has been reshaped several times in response to the needs and problems of business and the larger society. Indeed, many of the issues in the field's historical development continue to be salient today; in some ways they are the source of today's challenges but they are also, in some cases, windows into what will be needed to meet those challenges.

Chapter Three turns to the experience of today's undergraduate business students. We draw here not only on our conversations and observations at particular institutions but also on what is known through research and practice about the larger world of undergraduate business programs. Our findings point to the strengths of business programs—particularly their attention to students' application and use of knowledge in real-world contexts—and to limitations that call out for a more robust dose of knowledge, skills, and ways of thinking from the liberal arts and sciences. Our sense of these strengths and limitations reflects what we learned about the goals and attitudes of students in business and the arts and sciences as well.

Chapter Four sets out a normative model of liberal education, its goals, and its distinctive modes of thinking, which we identify as Analytical Thinking, Multiple Framing, and the Reflective Exploration of Meaning. Our aim is to show what these three modes entail and to illustrate how they complement and can be enriched by the forms of Practical Reasoning characteristic of professional education. This chapter also compares undergraduate business with other forms of professional preparation.

Chapter Five describes some of the ways that the dimensions of liberal learning described in Chapter Four are taught in the courses we observed and examines their relative prevalence in different areas of the curriculum and the experience of students. We want to provide concrete instances of how these learning goals are addressed by faculty in business and in the liberal arts and to give the reader a sense of which goals are well represented, which warrant increased attention, and what can be learned from practices now in place on campuses we visited.

Chapter Six focuses on pedagogical strategies that support the integration of liberal and business learning. We highlight a set of powerful pedagogies that are especially characteristic of undergraduate business education but we also look at some that are important but not widely experienced by business students. The chapter suggests that arts and sciences faculty have much to learn pedagogically from their colleagues in business schools, just as business faculty can benefit from teaching approaches more characteristic of the liberal arts.

Chapter Seven goes beyond individual courses and classroom practices to examine different curricular models that hold promise for linking business and liberal learning in a more complete and integrated whole. The chapter also suggests ways that the double helix curriculum can be reinforced by student advising, faculty development, out-of-class experiences, and a wider campus culture. In all of these, institutional intentionality and commitment are essential.

Chapter Eight explores two emerging themes in business programs: globalization and entrepreneurship. These themes provide fertile ground in which to connect business and liberal learning toward more effective preparation of business leaders as global citizens. The chapter suggests approaches to teaching for global competence and entrepreneurship, including social entrepreneurship, that tie these subjects closely to the content, goals, and practices of liberal education.

Chapter Nine considers the importance of rethinking business education and highlights five broad recommendations for change. Our emphasis is on the implications of our central thesis: that in order to add value in contemporary business settings and contribute as well to the larger world, students need a stronger education in the liberal arts and sciences, one that is intentionally integrated with their preparation for a career in business. The book concludes with a number of practical action items that can help campuses get started with a process that is necessarily long term but also urgent.

A Teachable Moment

The need to broaden the focus of undergraduate business education today struck us with particular force in part because of the timing of our research. We were in the process of visiting campuses when the economic crisis began in 2008. As the crisis deepened and grew in scope, we found ourselves in the midst of a teachable moment, with the stage set for extensive analysis and debate about the causes of the disaster, how to respond, and what would prevent its repetition. Why did this crisis happen and on such a scale? Who did what? How is it like and unlike other economic catastrophes, such as the Great Depression? What do we mean by a successful economy and how can we determine soundness? What role should business professionals play in ensuring economic success? And, of course, what should be done next and who should do it?

Such questions represent a great opportunity for business programs, a chance to validate the worth of business in the academy by bringing the analytical tools of the business disciplines to bear on the causes and dimensions of the crisis. Professions such as medicine and engineering focus a good deal of attention on understanding failures as ways to improve future practice (Cooke et al., 2010; Sheppard et al., 2009). Here, it seemed, was a parallel opportunity for business to examine its own thinking, its models and mind-sets, its strengths, and, yes, its failures and shortfalls.

Certainly we saw some of this kind of reflection and soul searching. In Chapter Five we tell the extended story of how one program seized the moment for self-reflection and reform. But, to put it frankly, in most cases this potentially teachable moment seems to have been a missed educational opportunity.

What we expected to see was urgent attention within business programs to probing such a frightening, large-scale catastrophe, one that threatened to destroy the global economic system itself. Instead, in many of the sites we visited, the crisis was characterized as a kind of natural event, like being overtaken by a storm, which was unforeseeable and perhaps inexplicable. In classes we observed, there was little systematic, disciplined examination of the institutional context and public policies that underlay the events.

This was surprising, especially considering the repeated crises of the previous decade. The crash of the dot.com boom in 2000, followed by the Enron and WorldCom failures in 2001—each of which caused huge losses of assets—had already revealed dangerous weaknesses in accounting, managerial, and investor practices throughout the economy. At least within the scope of our observations, it seemed that although students and faculty felt overtaken by events, relatively few were motivated to examine deeply how an economic meltdown of this magnitude could have occurred. Many we spoke with seemed to hope that it would all somehow be corrected so they could resume business as usual. Their previous understandings of the workings of the business world were so strong that, even in the face of massive problems, neither business faculty nor students cracked open those understandings to reveal the need for alternative points of view and new approaches.

At the same time, it should be said that the largest business event of our times raises questions not only about undergraduate business education but also about undergraduate education as a whole. An educationally coordinated approach to understanding the crisis must engage the liberal arts and sciences along with the business disciplines. The failure to provide coordinated settings and experiences in which students could engage with a signal event of the time reveals not only narrowness in the business fields but also insularity in the arts and sciences.

Additionally, this missed opportunity underscores the pressing need to revise undergraduate education to ensure that when students graduate they are on the path toward becoming fully reflective business professionals and not simply technicians. The great strength of U.S. higher education, its comparative global advantage, has been its commitment—most visible in liberal education—to providing undergraduates with a broad understanding of the world, encouraging them to probe and link ideas for deeper understanding. In the world of technological competition, this has been hailed as the key strength that U.S. institutions can build on (National Academy of Engineering, 2004). We believe that business education could strengthen these same qualities by integrating liberal learning with business preparation toward a higher level of performance.

○

It is not perhaps altogether surprising that the teachable moment of the 2008 financial crisis has so far been turned to little immediate educational advantage. Learning from failure is not easy; lessons need time to sink in, to filter through the system, to generate alternative ways of thinking and acting. Perhaps, too, the crisis represented too great an intrusion on some of the key assumptions of recent business theory. However, like business itself, business education must continually improve its capacity for learning and change.

As we will say more fully in the chapters that follow, business preparation in the United States faces new uncertainties and complexities. It seems abundantly clear, for example, that the business sector will become increasingly interrelated with government, not-for-profit, and scientific research sectors, especially as business comes to operate in an ever more international context.

Within this global perspective it also is becoming clear that the conditions governing the conduct of business have become less stable than the current, highly technical model of business education presumes. As a result, there will be increased demand for skill in understanding and negotiating varying social environments. This in turn demands breadth and flexibility of mind among business professionals, precisely the qualities that have long been objectives of liberal education.

For these reasons, we believe that the time has come to reimagine undergraduate business programs. Our investigation is intended as a contribution to that venture.

2

BUSINESS AND
THE ACADEMY

FOUNDING HOPES
AND CONTINUING CHALLENGES

WE UNDERTOOK THIS STUDY at what has turned out to be an inflection point for U.S. business and the global economy. The effects and implications of the Great Recession that began in 2008 have yet to fully work themselves out but it is already clear that those events have created a kind of watershed, casting doubt on taken-for-granted assumptions about the way business and the global economy should operate. More than ever before, business leaders face a complex and fragile interdependence that affects all participants in the global economy, and it is ever more obvious that actions providing immediate advantage to some cannot be counted on to benefit all. In short, these new times raise questions about widespread business practices, the meaning of leadership and expertise, and, ultimately, the very purpose of business.

These questions create challenges for business education as well. Today's conditions make even more important the preparation of business professionals who have a wide-ranging and versatile understanding of the world. Much as the imperative of sustaining a viable environment demands attention to the interconnection of human and natural processes, the future of business requires leaders who can think strategically not only about the advantage of the firm but also about the effects of business activity on other sectors of society, including government, education, culture, and communities. This strategic thinking requires the ability to understand how those sectors constrain or support business and, critically, how to engage with those social sectors to sustain the larger-scale environments on which the flourishing of business depends.

To achieve these ambitious goals, it is critical that women and men in business perform not simply as technicians but also as committed professionals, comparable to the best representatives of medicine, engineering, and the law. This imperative is hardly new. Indeed, when it comes to the themes of this book, the past may well be prologue, for it turns out that the need to inculcate in its graduates a concern for the effects of their activities on the well-being of society as a whole was a seminal issue in the field's founding a century ago. In this chapter, we review that founding and the history of reform in business education as well as shifts in the character and conduct of business itself, reflecting on the implications of both for the integration of liberal learning and business education.

Business Comes to the Academy

Business education in the U.S. university has an identifiable starting point, an institutional location, a founder, and a clearly stated purpose. The year was 1881, the place was the University of Pennsylvania, and the founder was the Philadelphia Quaker steel and nickel manufacturer, Joseph Wharton, a major leader in business and civic affairs of the time. Along with a large gift, Wharton persuaded the university to establish a new kind of school for undergraduates alongside existing departments and disciplines. His aim was to replace the ad hoc nature of on-the-job business training with systematic cultivation of a perspective that would combine courses in the knowledge and arts of "modern finance and economy" with the broadening effects of the liberal arts, including a special focus on the then-new social sciences of economics and politics. In his sociological history of U.S. business schools, Rakesh Khurana emphasizes that Wharton envisioned nothing less than the "creation of a new class of university educated businessmen" who "would be an amalgam of the professional and the man of affairs, similar to the civil service ideal that captivated so many of Wharton's contemporaries . . . [able to] use the 'social science' and vocational training offered in the new Wharton course to manage practical problems" (Khurana, 2007, pp. 106–108, quoting Steven A. Sass on Wharton).

The Wharton School was therefore attempting a kind of integrated liberal education for business in order to shape a new kind of highly educated man of affairs. This was happening at the same time that other universities were attempting to establish new kinds of education for the established professions of medicine and law while bringing additional occupations such as engineering into the university orbit. This movement to professionalize occupations and to base training for those fields in the emerging institution of the research university was one of the epochal developments of the end of the nineteenth century in the United States. Although less immediately successful than medicine or law in establishing itself as a profession, business made great strides through the efforts of visionaries such as Joseph Wharton and the Harvard Business School's dean, Wallace B. Donham. As Khurana notes, "The new American university granted many existing and incipient occupational groups a locus for attaining such collective consciousness and initiating collective action . . . a commonality . . . derived from the common experience of higher education . . . endowing these professionalizing occupations with the moral authority and sense of purpose inherited from the university's own founding logic. This sense of more-than-instrumental function attends the traditional professional's performance of his or her occupational role . . . the university transformed the pursuit of secular knowledge into . . . a *calling*" (p. 84, italics in original).

The Movement Toward Professionalization

The ideal guiding these movements to professionalize has been characterized as a social trusteeship. As did the civil service ideal that attracted Wharton, this concept meant that professions stood for the conscientious performance of key social functions, such as civil order and justice, health, or education, and that their members therefore had a high responsibility to practice their craft in the most enlightened way possible— hence the importance of university training—with the public welfare as guiding purpose (Brint, 1994; Sullivan, 2005). Admittedly, the ideals of professionalism were far from the only forces at work in this movement toward professionalization; efforts to professionalize management often reflected a concern with boosting the status (and therefore the income) of managers with university training (Bledstein, 1976; Larson, 1977). It is significant, however, that business education began as an effort to establish university training as a way to instill in the then-new occupation of manager an understanding of purpose that was explicitly public in orientation. For this purpose an education based in the liberal arts was thought essential.

But what was it about the world of business that led these founding figures to leap beyond the customary idea of apprenticeship in a counting house, bank, or enterprise as preparation for business? The business world Joseph Wharton and his associates were responding to—and had helped to create—was marked by vast economic transformation.

By the end of the nineteenth century, giant new institutions—industrial corporations such as General Electric, Carnegie Steel, and Rockefeller's Standard Oil—were able to dominate whole industries, providing themselves with buffers from the daily insecurities of market competition facing small businesses. This in turn enabled corporations to develop expensive new technologies whose efficiencies eventually provided even more growth and profitability. It was this new business institution that gave rise to the demand for managers. The idea was to replace the original robber barons' swashbuckling, sometimes bloody competitive drive toward monopoly with a more civilized form of enterprise, still innovative but responsive to the needs of the company's workers and the larger society. The hope was that the professional manager would be equipped and motivated to administer and develop the resources of the great enterprises in much the way other professionals were expected to function in fields such as the law, medicine, education, and journalism (Chandler, 1977).

This set of hopes and developments was background for the gestation of business education in the university. Indeed, U.S. universities were undergoing something of a managerial revolution of their own at this time, with increasingly specialized faculties managed by administrative personnel responsible to a chief executive officer, who in turn served at the pleasure of a board of trustees. Many of these trustees and much of the new universities' financial support came from the same large businesses and successful businessmen. Meanwhile, spurred in part by labor unrest, citizen protests against corporate abuse sought to civilize, even to moralize, the practice of business. College education for business personnel fit well into this atmosphere of reform.

At the same time, the circumstances that led managers to identify with their firms also worked against their sense of themselves as an independent profession defined by its civic responsibilities. Although some expressions of social trusteeship might be expected of corporate leaders, most managers sought to be effective business technicians, often with specific expertise in defined areas such as accounting, finance, engineering, or marketing. Their paramount purpose was to make the company work as efficiently as possible to enhance its strategic position and reward its investors. In companies that developed out of the new technologies of the era, the engineering impulse toward greater efficiency and productivity in the use of resources, especially human resources, seemed a natural way to think about the goals of the firm. And in this climate, public purposes could often remain matters for official pronouncements and public relations—not coincidentally, another new industry invented during this period.

Split Image: The Unresolved Problem of Professional Knowledge for Business

During the early years of business education in the university, the nature of the managerial profession itself had become contested terrain. The aspiration toward management as a publicly oriented profession of economic stewardship jarred against the equally compelling concept of the manager as technical expert, an image in keeping with the rule-governed, utilitarian qualities of corporate life. Some reformers of the era, such as Frederick Winslow Taylor, pushed the second option, arguing that more scientific ways of organizing work would solve the problems of social polarization that stalked the early twentieth century United States. Other notables, including Louis Brandeis, concurred, seeing in Taylor's new science of management a route to enhanced social equality, because more effective production promised greater general prosperity. Advocates of the civic ideal of professionalism, such as Herbert Croly, countered that the crucial need was for managers who could harmonize conflicting goals of profit and social responsibility within the fast-changing business context. In the view of these advocates, economic efficiency was a means rather than a goal unto itself, and one that had to be recalibrated in the light of changing social ends (Sullivan, 2005).

In this debate, the stakes for business education were high. If taken as a serious goal in education for business, understanding and balancing strategic goals with social responsibilities would require strong ties to liberal education precisely in order to ensure that future managers could grasp the complexities of multiple aims and conflicting interpretations of facts. In contrast, if economic efficiency and technical productivity were the only or dominant goals, then preparation for management could more narrowly focus on technological and economic competence. This split image of the identity of professional management posed a problem for business education, one that has remained unsettled, as we will describe in subsequent chapters.

It soon became clear that the new university schools of business were only partly able to make good on their intention to develop the kind of knowledge and training that could provide powerful guidance for the manager as a professional social trustee. Without a distinctive kind of professional knowledge, analogous to that of the lawyer, physician, or professor, the manager would inevitably be defined by whatever the company construed management's job to be. Business educators thus faced the same challenge all educators for the modern professions were obliged to take up: to bring the analytical and conceptual resources of the university to bear on the sorts of craft knowledge embodied by the best practitioners in their particular fields, and to raise idiosyncratic rules of thumb to the level of general principles supported by evidence.

In so doing, the pioneers of medical and legal education hoped to make their experts' understanding more comprehensible and publicly available for aspirants to those fields. At the same time, they sought to improve performance within the field through careful instruction, mentoring, and practice based on the development of expert knowledge and skill. Through involvement of the academic disciplines, it was believed that the university setting would encourage a deeper understanding of the context and nature of the profession's knowledge and practice.

The contribution business schools could make to management as a profession, then, would be to develop a kind of expert knowledge parallel to that being sought for the guidance of other professions. The unresolved question concerned the kind of knowledge needed to underwrite that aim, and the answer was what might be called *normative practical knowledge* for business. Such knowledge differs from theoretical knowledge in the usual scientific sense: facts and principles discovered by investigation that is itself free of moral significance and value, such as the concept of gravitational attraction in physics or the principles of chemical transformation. Knowledge of this kind derives from taking the position of an observer of events, charting their movements, and searching out their causes. It is knowledge gained from observing from the outside.

By contrast, normative practical knowledge entails engagement. It is knowledge gained from observing from the inside, usable by actors pursuing purposes within complex social relationships. In other words, unlike purely scientific knowledge, this is an understanding shaped by the meaning events have for agents in specific contexts, such as whether the events spell profit or loss or whether they reflect well or badly on the ethical or other qualities of the agents.

The major issue for all kinds of normative practical knowledge, then, is how to judge and act appropriately in the situation at hand. The kinds of questions this prompts are essentially those of interpretation, issues that inevitably involve moral decisions: given who I am, for what and to whom am I responsible? What do these obligations mean, concretely, in this present situation? Answering questions such as these requires an understanding of who we are, what our situation actually is, and where we stand within an overall scheme of relationships and connections.

Professionals must also engage with their clients to define ambiguous problem situations before they attempt to solve them. Because these situations will vary in myriad ways, professional procedures can be codified—made into explicit techniques—only up to a point. Beyond that, and even for deciding *when* to use a given technical routine, judgment is required. This introduces an inevitable tension into professional practice, and today there are continuing disputes within fields such as medicine about the proper use and scope of formal procedures in ways that support and improve rather than undercut professional judgment. The tension is clear: professional knowledge is ultimately of a practical rather than theoretical kind but practice is inherently fallible and uncertain, no matter how certain the facts or principles underlying the practice. In short, it is the cultivation of good judgment, such as that found in the expertise of a good physician or attorney, that is the aim of normative practical knowledge—and of professional education.

The hope of the pioneers of business education was that the new social sciences, the discipline of accounting, and the study of business experience could provide firm facts and principles (an outside point of view) to draw on in developing expert professional judgment (the inside point of view) in managers. But the ultimate educational aim, the cultivation of managerial judgment, required the student's ability to interpret the human meaning of the facts discovered by social science and to do so within changing situations. Such interpretation, as pioneers such as Wharton intuited, was the special province of the humanities and other liberal arts fields. But for professionals, developing judgment and acquiring normative practical knowledge can occur only by the student's adopting the moral perspective of the responsible practitioner. The analogy business education was implicitly drawing on here was to clinical training in medicine or to learning legal judgment. Indeed, the famous case method introduced into graduate business education at Harvard Business School by Dean Donham was adapted from the Harvard Law School's famous case-dialogue pedagogy (Garvin, 2003).

In the contentious environment of the early twentieth century business world, however, there was no clear agreement about what those responsibilities were. There was even less consensus about the human meaning and moral significance of the functions of either the manager or the business firm. These were, as they still are, contested issues of political and social import, not straightforward questions of empirical fact. By leaving those questions unresolved, however, business schools were handicapped. They could not fully develop the normative practical knowledge on which the professionalization of management depended. The default position became the idea of management as procedure, practiced by managers able to use increasingly sophisticated techniques of decision, measurement, audit, and accountability. Such training could sidestep the question of how to teach *complex practical reasoning* (to use a term we will discuss in Chapter Four) of the kind described as *leadership*. Although business practice might in fact depend on such skills, they were far less prominent in business education (Kanter, 1977).

The continuing challenge for business educators, then, is to resist the tendency to subordinate the complex task of training judgment to the simpler task of developing students' proficiency in using conceptual techniques to solve technical problems. The latter is very important, certainly, but business professionalism, the normative practical knowledge described previously, demands more—and in particular it demands teaching the arts of balancing and reconciling sometimes inherently contrary aims. It means doing justice to the various participants and interests represented in and affected by business activity. This has become all the more important as business has evolved to become ever more intertwined with other spheres of contemporary life.

Trouble in the Academy

The difficulties resulting from the dominance of the bureaucratic form of the corporation, which tended to subordinate normative practical knowledge and judgment to formal procedures and rules, was not the only challenge to the development of business education as a fully professional field. There was also a powerful trend of criticism and hostility from *within* the academy. The early twentieth century university had added to the earlier American college the superstructure and aims of a research institute, modeled on German universities. Whereas the nineteenth century college had been a teaching institution emphasizing a traditional arts and sciences curriculum integrated by a moral philosophy course, the research university came to equate academic excellence with the rigor of the research enterprise. Harvard, Yale, Princeton, and most U.S. universities had, by this time, developed from such colleges, reinventing themselves as amalgams of the older college and the new research departments. The first of these was, however, the Johns Hopkins University, endowed by a successful industrial entrepreneur in order to promote the modern research ideal.

In 1930, Abraham Flexner, a famous graduate of Johns Hopkins who had previously distinguished himself by urging the reform of medical education to ground practice in scientific research, sharply attacked the inclusion of business in the university. In his influential study, *Universities,* Flexner assailed modern business as distinctly less than a profession. "It is shrewd, energetic, and clever," he wrote, "rather than intellectual in character; it aims—and under our present social organization must aim—at its own advantage, rather than noble purpose within itself," as do true professions such as law, medicine, and teaching (Flexner, 1930, p. 164).

Moreover, Flexner argued that because business fields neither generated nor taught independent knowledge of their own, "undergraduate schools of commerce or business" such as those at universities like Chicago or Columbia were "poor substitutes for a sound general college education and in the long run would seem likely to be of little importance even from a vocational point of view" (p. 162). Although Flexner thought there was every reason to "study the phenomena and problems of business" through economics or sociology, it was outside the university's legitimate purview to try to "short-circuit experience" to provide functionaries to modern corporations through curricula keyed to business preparation (p. 165).

Flexner's critique summarized his contemporaries' standard objections to including business schools at the undergraduate level and he anticipated most of the objections that would later be made to the academic quality and value of business courses. In this, he certainly had a point. With few formal disciplines (aside from accounting, which had both a rigorous method and professional certification procedures), business programs were often staffed largely by retired business people who had little interest in academic standards of instruction or research. Indeed, graduate programs in business developed in many places during this period precisely because, as at Harvard and Dartmouth, the faculty refused to recognize business as a valid academic pursuit for an undergraduate degree (Khurana, 2007). Moreover, students in business programs were notorious for their indifference to either academic achievement or the higher aims espoused by the leaders of many of the schools, a condition epitomized by the announced student aim "to make a million before I'm thirty" (Khurana, 2007, p. 181).

Even so, the drive to professionalize business continued, led more often by academic leaders than by business itself. While Flexner was attacking business education as anti-intellectual, no less an intellectual figure than Harvard philosopher Alfred North Whitehead rose to its defense as a legitimate, even an important, area for study and teaching in the university. Asked in 1928 by Dean Wallace Donham to address the twenty-fifth anniversary celebration of Harvard Business School's founding, Whitehead pointedly associated the Business School with the university's other professional schools, arguing that they shared a critical purpose. Such schools were central to the university's social mission, he argued; they nurtured creative contexts wherein conceptual imagination and intellectual rigor, derived from the university's core traditions, could intersect the practical passions of human flourishing.

"The conduct of business," Whitehead asserted, "now required intellectual imagination of the same type as that which in former times passed into those other occupations [law, clergy, medicine, science]. . . . The justification for a university is that it preserves the connection between knowledge and the zest for life." In what Whitehead called "the complex modern social organism," the "adventure of life cannot be disjoined from the intellectual adventure" (Whitehead, 1967, pp. 92–95). The challenge, he went on to note, lay in making positive use of the potentially damaging tension between the needed focus on particular goals such as profit in business, on the one hand, and, on the other, imaginative sensitivity to how the special interests of business can contribute to the values of human civilization in all its dimensions. This was a description of the defining purpose of a business education that could meet Flexner's criticism head on.

An Upgrade: Inventing the Business Disciplines

The Great Depression of the 1930s muted this debate within higher education. With business, especially Wall Street, widely perceived as the villain responsible for global economic collapse, some business school leaders saw a teachable moment, ripe for self-criticism and improvement. In this spirit, they wondered publicly if they were doing enough to provide business personnel with more than narrow, self-interested skills and aims (Khurana, 2007).

Unfortunately, such reflection was short-lived as U.S. victory in World War II changed the subject and ushered in the most prosperous period in the nation's history—nearly three decades during which productivity per hour rose more rapidly than ever before or since. The new social arrangements that sustained this remarkable period of growth centered on a loose partnership between an expanded national government and business, which occupied a new, more positive role as the champion of national prosperity.

At the core of the new order was the idea of expert management. During World War II, a whole series of new scientific methods was developed that allowed for far more effective control of large-scale processes than had ever been possible before. Known collectively as *operations research*, these new, highly mathematical disciplines proved effective in raising the efficiency of industrial as well as military and technological activities. The new ideas centered on quantitative analysis of processes and the design and control of systems of production, distribution, accounting, and overall operations. In the 1960s, Robert McNamara famously brought these new tools of management from the Ford Motor Company to the U.S. Department of Defense. In the business realm, the aim of these systems of expert management was to boost efficiency by reducing the uncertainty that hampered effective planning and control of corporate activity. As much as possible, this new approach to management aimed to replace interpretation and qualitative judgment with formal, quantitative processes of information processing and decision making.

In this heady atmosphere of growth and prosperity, the university too underwent rapid and extensive expansion. From an elite institution that enrolled fewer than 15 percent of the nation's youth in the 1940s, higher education had by the 1970s become a mass sector, enrolling up to half of the age cohort. In the process, however, the educational values to which it gave prominence also changed. Elite education had aimed at preparing already privileged or especially talented, largely white, Protestant young men for leadership roles in society. After World War II, the older liberal education model continued but it remained identified with the academy's earlier elite aims and mission. By contrast, higher education as a whole began shifting during the postwar decades toward the preparation of much larger numbers for more specialized, technical occupations, with business among the main growth areas (Cheit, 1975; Trow, 1973).

Higher education was also seeking to upgrade itself during these years, reshaping its priorities to support the kinds of research that attracted federal funds. During the late 1950s and early 1960s, prestigious national foundations, especially the Ford Foundation, turned their attention to improving the teaching but especially the research carried on by business faculty. In order to measure up to the more scientific academic standards, business schools were encouraged to reorganize around four specific areas: economics and finance, accounting, marketing, and general management.

Along the way, new departments in these fields were established to develop PhDs who could meet the standards for scientific research being set by the social sciences. Such research, it was generally believed, had to move away from the attention to context and history that marked much of the older writing about business in order to produce more quantitatively respectable scientific knowledge. The research ideal also pointed toward a greater emphasis on graduate as opposed to undergraduate business education. Thus, in the public as well as the academic mind, the masters of business administration virtually defined the field (Khurana, 2007), as it continues to do today in most settings. An unintended consequence of these developments—one with which this book is centrally concerned—was to distance the business disciplines from the humanities and qualitative social sciences and from the tradition of undergraduate liberal learning.

Voices for Reform

Over time, these trends prompted intense critical inspection. The chief instruments that promoted change were two reports, both published in 1959, that were intensely critical of business programs as they were then. Carnegie Corporation of New York released *The Education of American Businessmen: A Study of University-College Programs in Business Administration*, authored by Frank Cook Pierson. Simultaneously, the Ford Foundation issued *Higher Education for Business* by Robert Aaron Gordon and James Edwin Howell. Both reports emphasized the rising numbers of business undergraduates, their demographic diversity, and, compared to arts and sciences majors, the lower educational and economic attainments of their families. The reports also emphasized business students' typically marginal academic achievement. Similar comparisons showed business program faculty to be less academically credentialed than their arts and sciences peers and business programs to be highly uneven in their degree of academic rigor. All this added up to a serious indictment of the academic quality of undergraduate business schools and programs.

Needless to say, the reports elicited a great deal of comment, criticism, and debate. In fact, one might say that 1959, and not 1930, was the year that Abraham Flexner's critique of business education bore fruit. In the end, even the American Association of Colleges and Schools of Business (AACSB—later called the Association to Advance Collegiate Schools of Business) accepted the criticisms and endorsed the reports' suggestions for reform. These centered on upgrading faculty training and credentials, and so reinforced the Ford Foundation's commitment to developing rigorous academic standards for the four business disciplines.

But the reports also insisted that business students spend more time studying the arts and sciences. The purpose in this was different from ratcheting up the rigor in the new business disciplines. Rather, the liberal arts were seen as a way to enhance students' capacities for analytical thinking, problem solving, and judgment while also developing their abilities to work together and to lead. The intent was not to segregate business from broader thinking but to realize Alfred North Whitehead's vision of business education as a creative infusion of imagination and rational argument into learning the practical affairs of managing enterprise. In practice, however, the recommendation to include more liberal arts came to mean academic curricula with the barbell shape described in Chapter One—with business disciplines and training on one end and liberal arts and sciences fields at the other. The intertwining of liberal arts thinking and business practice required to realize these hopes was simply too underdeveloped at that time to allow real integration.

Fifty years later, this lacuna must be seen as a serious failure of the pedagogical imagination at a crucial inflection point in the development of business education. Despite the good intentions of 1959, the unintended consequence has been the conceptually disjointed experience of liberal learning endured by so many undergraduate business students today.

When the Market Is the Mind-Set

If the postwar decades saw the apotheosis of management as a scientific system for guiding business and national growth, the period since the 1970s has been marked by the second coming of the nineteenth century's faith in laissez-faire and self-correcting markets. The economic shocks of the 1970s permanently destabilized the growth formula in the United States and the world economic order it had superintended. Although scientific management could coexist with (and even draw support from) the tacit moral order of company loyalty and business statesmanship, the revival of market thinking from the 1980s onward put pressure on the social trustee model of business professionalism. After 1980, the triumphal narrative that had sustained the Cold War added a new theme. The paladin of progress was no longer cooperation between corporations and government but the engineering of efficient markets. To this end, extensive deregulation of business and finance became national policy, first in the United States and then gradually around the world. Labor was left to fend for itself as new technologies of transportation, communication, and control spread rapidly as well.

These new technological developments, along with changes in business institutions, set in motion another epochal transformation in the way business is organized. The resurgence of confidence in deregulated markets and heroic self-reliance appealed to many in business who found themselves suddenly struggling amid the new conditions. The U.S. corporate elite of the postwar era who worked to accommodate and balance industry and finance with government and labor for long-term prosperity seemed no longer to represent the future (Mizruchi, 2010). The dominant form of the corporation, and therefore the conditions of work for business personnel, underwent dramatic reengineering. Outsourcing, for instance—contracting outside firms to produce component parts of a manufacturing process that is orchestrated by a larger, integrated company—had long been a staple of the industrial economy. But new electronic communications and more efficient shipping have made possible an exponentially larger and more complex system of global outsourcing.

Today, competitive advantage has swung to companies who can manage their supply chains, now often global in reach, in the most cost-efficient manner. Newer manufacturers, such as Dell Computers, make nothing in-house. Rather, they develop and market product lines based on intricate and fast-innovating supply chains that reach literally around the globe. This has become possible only because the complex tasks of production, finance, and marketing of rapidly evolving product lines can now be managed through information technology systems. In turn, this flexible new mode of production has required new ways of thinking about operations and strategy. The increased competitive pressure of deregulated, international markets has led firms to flatten the once vertically integrated ranks of management, often shrinking their core operations to the personnel of a small, strategically oriented central office.

In deregulated markets, economic efficiency can operate without social constraint. Production logically follows the slope of labor costs, increasingly to low-wage nations such as China. The result has been a great jump in the rate of return on capital invested in such innovative supply-chain companies. Consumer prices, too, have fallen. In such conditions, companies must compete strenuously for investment funds, which, thanks to financial deregulation, can now instantly go anywhere there is promise of a higher return. It is thus no coincidence that banking, insurance, and the financial sector generally have grown, become more concentrated, and now occupy the dominant position in the contemporary business world. The demand everywhere is for increased short-term return on investment, with few longer-term interests considered.

A business environment dominated by this kind of global financial activity has a natural affinity for the picture of the world generated by leading forms of contemporary economic thought. Neoclassical, highly mathematized economics has developed powerful if limited models that can explain and to some degree predict behavior under carefully specified constraints. Its core premise is the notion of the rational competence of self-interested actors. This means that individuals are assumed to act in ways that further their interests or "utilities," and that, given access to factual knowledge, individuals will choose the course of action most likely to advance their interests most effectively. Thus, if an observer can specify someone's interests accurately, it becomes possible to predict that individual's behavior. Markets, in this theory, become the preferred matrix for rational human interaction and decision making. Given accurate information about relative utilities as transmitted through the price mechanism, which is assumed to be reliable and available to all in an ideal market, general satisfaction of interests is guaranteed—if, that is, there is no interference with the self-interested, competitive search by each individual for the most rational strategy for investing time, labor, and money.

Following the logic of neoclassical economics, the business firm itself is seen not as a social organization held together by a web of social relationships but as a temporary set of contracts among self-interested market actors who come together in search of individual advantage. This marks an important shift. What had once been viewed as organizational issues, often with a moral subtext, are now typically described in terms of economic strategy alone. The rewards of work are assumed to be extrinsic, or utilities of the individual. Firms are simply groups of self-interested actors, from investors to managers to workers, bound by a series of contracts.

These employment contracts are agreed to because they are considered to define the most mutually advantageous transactions between employers and employees that current market conditions allow. Because all these actors are assumed to be self-interested, they are believed to be trying to get as much utility as possible for the lowest possible price. There is no place for moral considerations in this view. Instead, each actor faces the problem of protecting the property constituted by others' productivity—as wages or profits—that he or she has acquired in exchange for resources invested.

The key problem becomes ensuring that employees do *not* do what economic theory says they inevitably *will* try to do: exploit their contract and the firm for their own advantage. The old model of reciprocal loyalty between company and employee has no purchase here. In its place, the market model dictates that investors must either bribe or threaten top managers to ensure that the investors' interests get served, not those of the managers. These managers, in turn, must do the same to their subordinates to prevent their employees from doing the same thing to them, and so forth. The contemporary economic vision of the corporation is a chilly one. And, as it becomes accepted not simply as an analytical device but also as reality, this picture of self-interested competition becomes a self-fulfilling prophecy. Once people believe that others are acting competitively on the basis of self-interest, they frequently judge themselves vulnerable unless they adopt the same strategy. So all of business, if not all of life, becomes a problem of what economists call *agency*: how most efficiently to ensure a fair return on the property each actor has invested in the series of transactions that make up the firm, with primary emphasis placed on the property of the stockholders as opposed to the possible property of other actors in the firm such as the workers.

As management theorist John Hendry has pointed out, markets are most effective for the short-term distribution of goods and services to those who want them now. Coordinating activities over time, maintaining stability, and building for the future requires organizations that can give weight to the nonimmediate and build cultures of mutual trust in order to accomplish common ends (Hendry, 2004). It is hard to imagine global business functioning for very long in the absence of attention to maintaining stability and building for the future. In this sense, the current troubles of the world economy, as critics have charged, may stem in no small part from blind trust in an exclusively economic view of business and the world.

Business Today and Business Tomorrow

One thing is clear. Current conditions are pushing to the fore, in a new configuration, the unresolved questions about the nature of management. They have also stirred up the long-debated issue of how best to prepare students to function productively and responsibly in such a context. In the face of today's increasingly competitive global business environment, it is significant that although the twentieth century's multidivisional, hierarchical corporate form has changed significantly, business is still carried on by organizations and not just by individual traders in the market. Even when the shots are called by algorithmic formula, success depends on the ability to execute the play on the ground, with actual people interacting with other persons, inside and outside the organization over time.

Within firms, the chief organizational innovation has been to simplify divisional structure and loosen up formal rules while devolving much decision making and initiative to work groups. These groups or teams function like social networks, temporarily bringing together a variety of persons with diverse capacities for specific projects. Unlike either financial decisions determined by formula or procedures established by rule books, much of the activity of teams requires flexibility and shared responsibility, which in turn depend on establishing and maintaining mutual trust. Teams must be organized and coordinated effectively and often quickly. All this depends on the ability of the team leader to maintain the confidence and cooperation of the group in order to focus effort on achieving a common purpose.

Today's business organization, and no doubt tomorrow's as well, is therefore likely to be more variegated than the old corporate structures. It may include a skeletal form of the old organizational structure, now become more flexible through the greater role of finance and the strategic acuity demanded by highly competitive markets. But the decisive factor is arguably management's ability to cultivate effective teams and networks of expertise whose members come to share an understanding of collective purpose and develop ways of learning from their experience. Cultivating the knowledge and skill this kind of leadership requires harkens back to earlier efforts to develop a professional normative practical knowledge appropriate for business. Today's business conditions put a premium on leadership that knows how to blend technical competence, conceptual capacity, and interpersonal, even ethical, dispositions (Hendry, 2006).

The sort of mind and disposition that succeeds best at these complex tasks has been characterized by Roger Martin, dean of the Rotman School of Management at the University of Toronto, as *integrative thinking*. From a study of exceptionally successful business leaders, Martin has distilled the qualities of thinking employed by these leaders, qualities that set them apart from the many also-ran competitors in their industries. More routine-focused managers tend to shun messy situations and seek to apply one-track solutions to problems, which often locks them into unproductive trade-offs among competing strategies. By contrast, Martin's integrative thinkers are able to keep a large, complex problem in mind while investigating its several parts. This is because these leaders can see patterns, connections, and relationships among different aspects of the problems confronting their company. Unlike purely linear thinkers who see only one-way causation, integrative thinkers have developed the ability to hold conflicting strategies and imperatives together at the same time. This capacity to find integrative solutions to problems created by the messy conjunction of conflicting opposites is a cardinal feature of a high-quality liberal education. Martin's discovery is that this is precisely the capacity that identifies the most innovative and successful business professionals (Martin, 2007).

O

Reform is never easy but business education has a rich history and a wealth of good ideas and leadership to draw on. Our method in this book is to bring reflections on the field's development from the last century together with insights from the study of contemporary business, such as Martin's identification of the central importance of integrative thinking, to draw from the best current understandings of learning and intellectual development, and at the same time document and explore our own firsthand experience with a diverse set of business programs. In the following chapter, we turn our focus to current practice "on the ground," using what we learned in our site visits to ask hard questions about what works, what falls short, and what is missing in the experience of undergraduate business students today.

3

ON THE GROUND

THE CHALLENGES OF UNDERGRADUATE BUSINESS EDUCATION

GOING TO COLLEGE CHANGES PEOPLE. Regardless of their age or stage in life, people's understanding of the world, themselves, and their sense of what is possible are affected by the experience of higher education (Pascarella & Terenzini, 2005). In these ways, higher education is a deeply *formative* experience for all those who undergo it. In our visits to undergraduate business programs around the country, we heard from business professors and faculty in the arts and sciences that students majoring in business stand out. Their prominent qualities include the ability to work in teams, enthusiasm for competition, and poise and preparedness in making public presentations. More than most undergraduates in general, many faculty reported, business students show a seriousness of purpose that manifests itself in the ability to manage time and effort efficiently.

These qualities are habits of mind and also of character. Students with these capacities seem to be predisposed to choose business as a field of study. However, the emphasis that many of today's business programs place on learning by doing through imaginative participation in business situations, simulations of business experience, and the development of actual businesses suggests that business programs are seeking to augment students' native potential with significant training and curricular reinforcement.

In our campus visits, we encountered a number of ways in which learning through experience has moved toward the center of business education. Many programs today seek to provide students with a vivid introduction to their future studies—and careers—that goes well beyond the typical beginning survey of the field. Rather than simply learning *about* the various aspects of modern business, these courses give students powerful *experiences* that approximate actual business thinking and practice; their engaging pedagogies share elements that have long been basic to professional preparation, especially supervised apprenticeships. At the same time, these courses emphasize analytical methods of the kinds taught in introductions to the four basic business disciplines of accounting, finance, marketing, and management.

In this sense, these introductory courses are hybrids in which the formal, analytical content of the core business subjects is presented in real or simulated contexts of operating—and sometimes even starting—a business. In attempting this, business programs embody an important, consistent finding of research on learning: that learning occurs most effectively when concepts and techniques are experienced not in abstraction but in context so that learners can immediately grasp the significance of key ideas or skills by applying them to realistic situations (Kuh, 2008). Not surprisingly, in the courses of this kind that we observed, students were highly engaged. Perhaps because they discovered that the concepts of the business disciplines could help them learn to function in a business setting, they showed strong motivation to master those disciplines.

In this chapter, we first take a look at the character and quality of learning in undergraduate business education "on the ground" as we observed it during our campus visits. Our questions here relate to the experience of students and especially the distinctive quality of that experience as a consequence of the field's orientation to learning by doing. Clearly, the courses and approaches we observed have important lessons to convey for business programs and the liberal arts and sciences—which could be strengthened by more attention to application and experience. But we will also look at what these approaches do *not* accomplish. Like many other fields—think of the case method in law, design experiences in engineering, and the seminar in various humanities fields—business has developed classroom approaches that are distinctly engaging but also (ironically because they may sometimes work *too* well) overly narrow and insufficient to cultivate the full range of outcomes needed by business professionals today and tomorrow (Shulman, 2005). Thus, in looking at both strengths and limits, we aim to flesh out our vision of a more integrated education that draws together business and liberal learning.

Deep Dives but a Narrow Pool

Consider, for instance, Contemporary American Business, a course required of all entering business majors in the Leavey School of Business of Santa Clara University, a comprehensive institution with a strong commitment to liberal education in the Jesuit tradition. Students also take introductions to specific business disciplines, but Contemporary American Business is designed to provide a sense of the whole of business as a field. As one instructor told us, "This is the launch of a student's business career." The many sections of the course are taught by adjunct faculty with business experience and led by a full-time professor who came to academe after a high-level career in the information technology industry.

Although the course includes standard classroom presentations and multiple-choice examinations focused on course content, one-third of the final grade depends on performance in a semester-long simulation. Called "Mike's Bikes," the simulation engages students in a complex, interactive, Web-based game similar to the experience of operating a chain of bicycle sales-and-repair shops. In the first half of the term, students become acquainted with the simulation and its underlying concepts by working as individuals. In the second half, they are grouped into five-person teams. The simulation, the instructor emphasizes, is very realistic in that what each team decides to do in a given round changes the competitive environment for all the other teams in the subsequent rounds. The situation thereby becomes progressively more complex and competitively charged.

The emphasis in Mike's Bikes is on formulating an overall strategy for a particular enterprise within a highly competitive environment. This requires intensive interaction among the marketing, production, finance, and accounting functions of each enterprise, which are typically the responsibility of different team members. It also requires a grasp of the evolving situation and the ability to arrive at complex strategic decisions. For example, although it is obvious that increased profits are likely to demand expanded production, this in turn requires financing, which depends on increasing sales and, if possible, raising profit margins on those sales. But actual revenue will also be affected by competitors' strategies, which may undercut well-formed plans and lead to unforeseen declines in volume or losses, entailing the need to rethink the entire strategy and maybe even change direction quickly. Over time, teams win or lose as the profitability of their enterprise rises and falls through rounds of play. At the end of the term, the team's grade depends on its relative ranking at the close of the competition.

The instructor we spoke with has clearly been pleased at the way the simulation makes basic business concepts come alive for the students. In his view it provides a "liberal arts" experience in that it gives the "broad exposure" that is the aim of a survey course. And certainly we were impressed with students' level of engagement, intellectual energy, and seriousness—qualities one wants to see in all aspects of a college education.

Additionally, the course plunges students imaginatively into a business environment. It teaches them how to take realistic roles in an ongoing enterprise. Students learn how to draw on a complex set of concepts and viewpoints rooted in the business disciplines in order to coordinate a management strategy. They get a feel for the challenges, excitement, and risks of such undertakings. Working in teams, they come to experience and learn about the importance of trustworthiness and ethical integrity to the functioning of actual businesses.

What was less clear was how the course, and in particular its most vivid component, Mike's Bikes, represents to the students the occupation and world of business. How does the world look from that point of view? What is valued? What kinds of dispositions characterize the typical winner in the simulation? Is this faithful to actual business life? Finally, how is success in the bicycle industry, or for that matter the success *of* the bicycle industry, related to the larger society? These were questions that did not surface in the discussion we observed. Thus, the simulation does a superb job of teaching students to link concepts with experience and motivating them toward their future studies in business but it does not provoke much critical thinking about the students' intended profession. It provides few conceptual tools that can help students think about this enterprise and its effects on themselves or on the larger society or world. Nor does it provide a larger moral or social framework within which students can explore the significance of what they are experiencing for themselves and for the world. In this sense, the chief virtue of the course is also its biggest limitation; it is deep but narrow.

Of course no class can do everything, but seeing the power of Contemporary American Business to engage students, we found ourselves wanting more—and wondering what enhancements might be possible. How might the distinctive strengths of courses like this and their commitment to learning from experience also make a space for reflection on business as an institution and on its important contexts or contributions?

Different Setting, Similar Story

Consider another example of an integrated freshman-year course designed to introduce students to the world of business. Babson College, all of whose students major in a business field, requires freshmen to spend two semesters in a demanding and intensely involving course called Foundations of Management and Entrepreneurship (FME). Babson students are academically strong and many seem confident and outgoing but the intensity and comprehensiveness of FME makes the course extremely challenging. It is intended to teach not only the four basic business disciplines—accounting, finance, marketing, and management—but also many practical business skills such as leadership, oral and written presentation, data analysis, problem solving, and teamwork. As the syllabus says, the stress throughout is on business as an integrative enterprise.

Faculty describe the first semester of the course as a boot camp, providing sessions on every aspect of business, including information technology, while students are also creating business plans and scouting possibilities for the actual business they hope to organize and run in the spring semester. This intensity creates a bond among first-year students, and FME is perceived by both faculty and students as a defining aspect of the student experience at Babson.

The latter part of the first term involves a competitive process in which each of twenty, three-person teams argues for a different business proposal. In successive competitive rounds, proposals are eliminated, transforming the group into two large teams with thirty members each. The selection of winning proposals is made by faculty on the basis of business plans supported by marketing surveys and focus groups, all of which the students learn to do as the experience unfolds.

In the spring semester, the two teams get their businesses up and running. All make use of technology and Web-based transactions, and they also engage in actual business activities. The students are organized into departments—such as sales, inventory control, finance, and even human relations, whose members have responsibility for motivating the efforts of other departments and for developing evaluation procedures for all personnel. Students do weekly presentations to the team. They must also succeed in two written examinations that ask them to apply the concepts learned in the various disciplines to the business they are running.

Another special feature of FME is its deliberate effort to teach social responsibility as well as business acumen. The course devotes lecture time and simulations to teaching about ethical issues, and ethical questions feature prominently in the feedback faculty give in response to student presentations. Each student volunteers for a nonprofit organization throughout the semester, and the two businesses form ongoing relationships with service organizations outside the college. Then, at the end of the spring semester, each team donates its profits to the organization with which it has affiliated, which adds to student motivation to succeed. The point, Babson faculty members told us, is to provide opportunities for students to contribute to the community even while they are learning to profit from selling products and services.

Compared to Santa Clara's Contemporary American Business, Babson's FME is a larger operation that runs for a whole academic year and involves an actual rather than simulated experience of running a business. FME also provides experience in management, in the operation of the business, and in entrepreneurship through students conceiving, researching, and starting a new enterprise. The community volunteering and social responsibility activities are also a step beyond what students do in the Santa Clara course. (It should be noted, however, that Santa Clara provides extensive encouragement and opportunities for social service in a variety of venues, though not in its introduction to business course.)

Yet, for all these differences, the aims and methods of the two courses are similar. Like the Santa Clara course, Babson's FME teaches students to apply their formal knowledge of the business disciplines in ways that require integration of the various parts. It also stresses team organization and relies on direct competition between teams as a source of motivation as well as a context for insight into what it takes to make an enterprise succeed. And, although community service is included within FME, those activities are fairly separate from the learning of business as an integrative enterprise. Social responsibility is therefore practiced to a significant degree as an activity outside and subsequent to business success. The relationship between the conduct of business itself, including its products and procedures, and the social and ecological surroundings of business do not figure as centrally in the shaping of social responsibility.

Making a Place for Critical Questioning

FME professor Steve Gordon emphasized that students learn a great deal in the course, including about social responsibility and ethics—and we agree. But, similar to his counterpart at Santa Clara, he believes that presenting business as an object of inquiry and critical questioning cannot be a central goal of the course, given how full the syllabus is already. In both settings, students have, after all, already chosen to pursue business as a career; providing them with tools that will enable them to succeed is understandably a high priority. Perhaps, then, business programs need to provide an additional, linked experience that could enable students, as citizens of a larger world, to focus squarely on the purposes, relationships, or responsibilities of business or of their business lives.

Here an objection naturally arises. Is not that kind of social and moral reflection properly the province of liberal education courses taught by arts and sciences departments, not a component of a business curriculum? All of the campuses we visited require their business undergraduates to take a considerable number of courses outside their major. Some of these are part of the schoolwide general education requirement that is intended to provide students with the kind of knowledge and skills that will enable them to ask—and answer—questions about the purpose and significance of what they are learning. However, although there are excellent examples to the contrary that we will discuss in later chapters, we discovered that it is typical for undergraduate business programs, like other majors, to require students to take two sets of courses: one in business and another defined by distribution requirements in arts and sciences disciplines. These two sets of courses are rarely coordinated with each other. Students may happen on connections among them, but there is nothing intentional in the program or structure of their coursework that ensures this or even makes it likely.

This problem is exacerbated and doubly unfortunate because many students—as we learned in talking with them in the settings we visited—interpret their business courses as the serious part of the curriculum, what they came for, and the distribution courses seem disconnected from their main interests and accordingly are given low priority. Students rarely come to see them as contributing importantly to their central educational aims. Especially when compared to the intrinsically engaging experience of introductions to their major such as those in FME or Contemporary American Business, liberal arts courses often seem pale or irrelevant.

Broadening the Frame: Business and Liberal Learning

The power of courses such as we observed at Santa Clara and Babson to shape students' understanding makes what is and is not included in business education a high-stakes decision. In these and other cases, we were impressed by well-conceived and effectively executed efforts at integration—and certainly by the power of experiential approaches to engage students' interest and effort. However, the question we posed to ourselves after our encounters with them, their faculty, and students was whether such courses provide a sufficiently broad foundation for students entering business as a field of university study.

The pedagogies of engagement that are rightly admired in business programs derive their power from the ability to present students with examples of desired identities as business persons and the intellectual and practical tools of the craft necessary to achieve those identities. Though this is not impossible (as examples later in this book will show) such pedagogies are rarely accompanied by comparable experience with modes of reflection on those identities and tools. Even less common is the inclusion of a critical approach that might provide the cognitive distance from which students could probe and question the larger significance of business and its institutions. Our point is that for many business majors, encountering intellectual resources that illuminate the larger significance of what they are learning remains very much a matter of curricular luck, be it in business courses or in the arts and sciences. In the latter, for instance, introductory courses are more often oriented toward recruiting majors into their departments than toward enabling students to draw on the conceptual resources of their disciplines to think about their studies in other subject areas, the larger world, or their lives beyond college.

This is disappointing because liberal learning has long been concerned with fostering just such capacities for reflection on purpose and identity. Indeed, that has been liberal education's chief reason for being. We will have more to say about the nature of liberal education in Chapter Four but we want to note here that as a tradition of learning it has sought to provide students with a vision of possibilities and the knowledge and capacities needed to sustain them.

Designing for Connections

Imagine, then, the difference it might make if students taking demanding introductions to business such as Contemporary American Business or FME were at the same time taking part in another course designed to provide reflection on the business experience from other disciplinary perspectives or a chance to explore a variety of perspectives on the responsibilities of business.

If these complementary courses were as compelling and high caliber as the best business courses, students would in effect be learning to understand the same situation from the viewpoint of different identities operating in differing social contexts. They would be learning to think in pluralistic ways. Linking business with arts and sciences courses in this way—through our double helix curricular model—could lay the groundwork for developing undergraduates' capacities as integrative thinkers from the beginning of their business study.

But why, then, is there often so little connection between these two vital aspects of business students' learning, so few efforts to provide integration? In seeking an answer we were struck by an insight from our discussions with groups of students and faculty. We set out to compare the viewpoints of business departments with those in the arts and sciences. In those conversations, we were repeatedly told that students in business programs were much more focused on succeeding than their counterparts in the arts and sciences. (This is not to say that this disposition is an exclusive preserve of business majors: premedical students and engineering majors, as our interlocutors agreed, also share these characteristics, as do some individuals in every field.) Accordingly, so runs the stereotype, business majors ask about every course: how will this help me get the grades I need and the knowledge and skills required for the highest-paying job possible on graduation? A primary criterion for whether to take an elective course, and of how much effort to expend on any course or assignment, is its literal cash value for one's future rate of compensation relative to the investment it requires. Students often describe the attitude underlying these tendencies as *instrumental*.

National data are consistent with this impression of business students as focused on the direct instrumental value of their studies. The National Survey of Student Engagement, for example, finds that business majors are less likely than students in most other fields to discuss ideas from their courses outside of class, to read books on their own for personal enjoyment or academic enrichment, or to attend cultural events such as art exhibits, plays, and music or theater performances (National Survey of Student Engagement, 2010).

Instrumental and Explorer Orientations

In contrast to this instrumental orientation, as our informants called it, arts and sciences majors (again excepting premeds, engineers, and other competitive preprofessional students) were seen and characterized themselves as motivated by intellectual and cultural curiosity. Such students were often described as treating their college experience as primarily an opportunity for *exploration*, calling themselves *explorers*. Used this way, *exploration* refers to intellectual pursuits not tied to getting a good job, admission to medical school, and so forth, and so is thought of as the polar opposite of an instrumental orientation toward study.

Although there is some truth in these stereotypes, such a stark dichotomy between preparing for a definite career versus intellectual exploration for its own sake replicates just the kind of division between the professional schools and the arts and sciences departments that works against the vision we are arguing for in this book. More important, accepting this dichotomy makes liberal learning a stepchild in its own house, caught between opposing, equally narrow views of higher education. These narrow conceptions of education miss what we believe is a better option—a path of coherent learning that opens possibilities for both intellectual exploration and vocational engagement.

The instrumental-versus-exploration dichotomy makes it hard for students—or their parents—to conceive of a college education that is both intellectually adventurous and yet serious, shaping a life that embraces responsible worldly endeavor but is also open to wonder and exploration. Absorption in the instrumental attitude risks closing students off to experiences of self-transcendence and transformation beyond immediate utility. It suppresses the big questions about what makes any career worthwhile and fails to stimulate creativity and thinking on a large canvas. Conversely, although an exploration orientation has virtues of openness, students with this orientation are often on the defensive in the face of messages that college is about getting ahead. This makes pursuing an exploratory course of study unappealing to those who are intellectually inclined but also aim to make something of themselves so they can contribute to the world.

There is plenty of evidence that what we encountered on our campus visits reflects a general attitude toward higher education today as an instrumental investment. The rising cost of college tuition, which has been a factor for some time, gives the push of necessity to the more general cultural drift in this direction. And the fact that these tendencies are particularly widespread among the largest group of undergraduate majors is, we believe, a warning sign. Although the more complex conditions of twenty-first-century business and life demand greater flexibility of mind and a broader understanding, the dynamics at work within American higher education are moving precisely in the opposite direction. The result is a serious national problem: higher education that is weak in a capacity that matters deeply, the ability to prepare citizens who both care about the world beyond themselves and have the wherewithal to contribute to it.

The Business Student Experience

Business students, then, experience college in ways that are heavily, even primarily, shaped by their hopes for a future career. They generally receive support in this from their families, their peers, and many of the professors and student services personnel on campus. In many ways, college changes business students much as it changes students in other majors. Nevertheless, at the end of college, business and engineering students still rate as significantly lower the importance of developing a meaningful philosophy of life, influencing the political structure, improving their understanding of other countries and cultures, and a number of related goals compared with students majoring in arts and sciences or most other professional fields. Business students also rate as more important being very well off financially along with other specifically business-focused objectives (Higher Education Research Institute, 2009). How can we explain these differences in outcome? To some extent, the differences between business and arts and sciences students are already present when students come to college but majoring in business during college certainly does not erase those differences.

The Business Curriculum

The typical undergraduate business curriculum is designed around coursework in the four main business disciplines: accounting, finance, management, and marketing. Some programs offer a bachelor of arts degree and others offer the bachelor of science. New or potential business majors generally take an introduction to business course, which provides an overview of the field. In the sophomore and junior years, majors typically take one or two courses in each of the core business disciplines and one or two courses in economics, mathematics, and business communication as well. In their junior and senior years, students typically take a concentration of three or four more advanced courses in their specific field. The senior year also frequently requires some form of capstone experience, often involving a significant team-based project. Additional courses on leadership, entrepreneurship, business ethics, business law, and other topics are common but they are not consistently required across business programs.

At the heart of this curriculum lie the four disciplines of accounting, finance, marketing, and management. As Chapter Two describes, these disciplines evolved as part of the modern MBA program, with its emphasis on scientific knowledge and rigor. The central place of the four disciplines, led by finance with its links to economics, was heavily promoted in the 1950s and 1960s by large investments from the Ford Foundation, one of whose aims was to rescue undergraduate business programs from the charge of being anti-intellectual—and to do so, intentionally or not, by making them mini-MBAs. Not surprisingly, then, undergraduate business courses are often taught by faculty who also teach in graduate programs.

Even more telling, few institutions with both MBA and undergraduate business programs differentiate the undergraduate curriculum enough to provide leadership by a separate dean (though the University of Virginia and New York University are exceptions). And some, such as Wake Forest University, are moving in the other direction, from separate undergraduate and graduate business schools to a single unified school.

As we suggest in Chapter Two, the contemporary form of undergraduate business programs is, in large part, the legacy of critical reports on undergraduate business education issued in 1959 by Carnegie Corporation of New York and the Ford Foundation (Gordon & Howell, 1959; Pierson, 1959). Those reports recommended more liberal arts instruction but their core focus concerned strengthening the business curriculum itself. At the time, the Ford Foundation was already significantly involved in reshaping the MBA through a coordinated strategy that included funding new PhD programs in the four disciplines and economics in order to produce a distinctive set of career tracks for business school faculty. It must have seemed logical to extend these efforts at professionalizing the business faculty to the undergraduate level. However, over time, as the increasing isomorphism of the MBA and undergraduate programs suggests, the distinctive purposes of collegiate education were eclipsed by the superior prestige (and funding) of graduate professional preparation in the business fields.

All of this has now come home to roost. As we heard many times from students, business education is focused on a clear goal: to acquire the knowledge and skills needed to function in business. Success is measured by the status—and remuneration—of the student's first job after graduation. (Unlike most other educational ranking systems, which emphasize institutional resources and reputation, *Business Week*'s influential scale emphasizes this last point as a criterion for the quality of business programs.) Today's business education is heavily cognitive in orientation and highly quantitative—an indication of how seriously academic undergraduate business education has attempted to become since the critical mid-twentieth-century reports.

Among the four business disciplines invented in the 1950s and 1960s, finance typically holds pride of place alongside economics, which is sometimes housed in the faculty of arts and sciences rather than the business school. In addition to drawing on the current intellectual prestige of economics, finance is of course also directly linked to the high-paying occupations of financial analyst and trader, which have been at the center of the latest phase of global business expansion (and subsequent collapse). The three other fields, accounting, marketing, and management, follow. The prestige hierarchy within business schools thereby reflects not only the job market but also, as the Ford Foundation's initiatives intended, the value the academy places on analytical, especially quantitative, training. One consequence is that social sciences other than economics along with the humanities figure less in the thinking of business faculty than they might if the markers of status were better related to understanding the complexities of contemporary business life.

A Market View of the World

These disciplines, including their relative prestige, also transmit a substantive view of the world that is important for understanding how business students are shaped by their education. Contemporary business programs present the market, as analyzed and idealized by economics and finance, as the key organizing structure. In this, they reflect important trends in the business world today. As vertically integrated manufacturing corporations such as General Motors have given way to more finance-driven production systems on the model of Walmart and Dell Computers, markets have grown in importance as mechanisms of coordination within as well as among firms. These developments have, in turn, identified the idealized market as *the* analytical framework within which the major problems and concerns of business are articulated.

Contemporary business is, in reality, far more than markets, however. It functions primarily by and through organizations that require other complex forms of social coordination, ranging from bureaucratic structures to interactive networks. In addition, all business firms, particularly those engaged in global webs of supply, are enmeshed in a variety of relationships with regulatory and licensing agencies of governments, unions, professional associations, and different types of communities. Yet, in our visits we found scarce attention to the discussion of government or other nonmarket modes of social organization that heavily influence the environment and conduct of business.

There are exceptions, certainly. Besides some integrative senior capstone courses, especially in management, the primary curricular site for these broader discussions is the area of business law. These courses often provide avenues through which students are encouraged to consider business as an institutional sector that influences, and is influenced and regulated by, other social sectors. Courses in law and business tend to require more reading and to provide more experience with extended writing assignments than most other business program offerings, and in this sense they help prepare students for the complexity of roles demanded by modern business enterprise. Typically, their faculty are drawn from outside the business disciplines, often from those with a background in legal practice or education. This, too, provides students with a broader exposure than do most courses in the business disciplines. Still, overall, the idealization of the market is pervasive and provides a kind of default perspective from which all questions are approached.

An idealized conception of the market also serves as a model for solutions to the problems of business and society. The disciplines of finance and economics have established a methodological premise that markets are ideally self-directed and self-correcting. Perhaps not surprisingly, the business students we spoke with viewed the expansion of market processes into new areas of social life as a positive development, seeming to take it as a given that competitive self-interest and strategic thinking are sources of greater efficiency and overall social benefit.

Within this framework, managers within corporations are also understood to be strategic actors working to further their own interests. The firms they manage are conceived primarily as vehicles for maximizing return to investors—their shareholders—whose interest is viewed as entirely strategic. And the idea of the business firm itself is often analyzed as a network of negotiated, marketlike transactions among various strategic actors. This *agency theory* of strategic management—as it is typically called—has spread from esoteric work in economics and finance to become a virtually self-fulfilling prophecy in business school teaching. It has weakened the legitimacy of older views of management as a profession with fiduciary relationships to various stakeholders, placing that view on the defensive. Indeed, we found that although few deans or faculty endorsed this "shareholder primacy" view, it appeared to be strongly entrenched in key parts of the curriculum.

Indeed, the theoretical ideal of social progress through market competition receives powerful reinforcement in the way business programs are structured. Undergraduate business education is highly competitive, with grading often on a strict curve. All of the programs we visited place significant value on academic achievement in the business disciplines and they also stress to students how the terms of this academic achievement reflect what business is like. Students work hard to master subjects and skills that are presented as "what you'll need to be able to do..." and it is this mastery that academic achievement is expected to confirm. Simulations and experiential courses, with all of their strengths, serve to amplify and reinforce these effects.

In this way, the market perspective that organizes most business coursework is enacted in the routines of student life. In many other fields, it is common to bemoan the ways in which the tacit or hidden curriculum of pedagogical and social practices contradicts or undermines certain explicit teachings of the formal curriculum. But we found business programs to present a very different picture: a tight congruence between the theoretical view of the world presented in core business courses, especially economics and finance, and the way students are encouraged to approach their education and, in fact, their future lives.

Philosophers since David Hume have inveighed against deriving prescriptive norms of conduct from descriptions of the way the world operates. But when the assumptions of economic theory are coupled to the notion that in the long run market competition is self-regulating and socially constructive, it is easy for students to slide from accepting the theory as an intellectual perspective into using it to define a complete worldview, one whose adoption promises both certainty and benevolent outcomes for all. In this regard, one of the most striking features of business programs we visited was their linkage of market theory with teaching practices that stress many of the same values described by the theory. In this sense, theory and practice are closely aligned. As students sometimes told us, eventually it becomes natural to think that "everything is business" and that the business aspect is the most important feature of any situation.

Preparation for Twenty-First-Century Business

As forms of corporate organization have changed, the effect for business education has been ever greater emphasis on narrower and more technical dimensions of business. The older type corporation, still enshrined in popular understanding, was a nationally based, vertically integrated organization that did everything in house and according to fixed procedures, from design through production to the selling of products and services. The successor type follows a different model: (1) a complex web of outsourced functions (2) organized by a central command function (3) into supply chains (4) whose intricate logistics are coordinated by information technologies that (5) allow quick response to market signals from all over the world. The increasing dominance of this type of organization has combined with other forces to focus business education's attention more intently on the quantitatively describable processes of logistical and market coordination. This shifting emphasis implies that these quantifiable processes capture the majority of what is most important in business. Only they don't.

This dominant technical model pushes into the background the institutional and social realities of business life. Although the aim of formal models in finance and economics is to make business operations more amenable to control, business organizations need more than market signals and sophisticated information technology in order to function. They also need legitimacy and purpose—among shareholders, in the eyes of the public, and, very important, for their employees—and this imperative has made operating a business more complex. For managers at all levels, today's companies are sites of complexity and uncertainty, moral ambiguities, and conflicts of values occasioned by the need to compete while also fostering cooperation within the organization. Meanwhile, the growing tide of criticism and hostility to unresponsive business power, at home and abroad, has raised the stakes for leadership. And none of these realities are adequately conceptualized, let alone addressed, by agency theory. Especially in today's advanced-technology industries, where knowledge is the key resource, it is the management of personnel that has emerged as the critical discipline. Organizations that can learn from experience to innovate in product design and organizational form depend heavily on the human capital of their workforces. Their success in releasing and harnessing this expansive form of capital requires, in turn, strong networks of social capital. This means that such enterprises demand subtle management of these networks of mutual trust. Under such conditions, it is impossible to disentangle purely instrumental techniques from the human, and therefore moral, relationships in which they are embedded and on which they depend for their effectiveness. Management in these cutting-edge sectors of knowledge-creation has become a form of leadership as much as or more than it is the application of technical disciplines (Heckscher & Adler, 2006; Hendry, 2004, 2006). To support innovation, business education will have to nurture mature practical judgment that can guide knowledge-intensive enterprise equitably for social benefit as well as profit.

Successful management of such organizations requires the kind of integrative thinking described by Roger Martin, whose work we invoke in Chapter Two: the ability to develop creative resolutions that reconcile seemingly conflicting approaches to pressing problems. The skills needed, according to Martin, can be described as a combination of opposites or what are often perceived as opposites. On the one hand, integrative thinking requires openness to complexity and awareness that any problem can be approached from several different perspectives—the sort of approach characteristic of the exploratory cast of mind we encountered among students in the liberal arts. But, on the other hand, effective business leadership also rests on mastery of the tools and instruments central to the business disciplines. The key educational experiences needed are, therefore, those that can strengthen *both* capacities of mind— learning situations that use practice guided by ongoing feedback to reinforce learners' ability to move back and forth between disciplined mastery of analytic tools and openness to other perspectives as they work to resolve a problem (Martin, 2007).

The key intellectual disciplines involved in this kind of leadership go beyond instrumental technologies and logistical programs, however important these may be. The essential knowledge that students will need in order to make sense of this emerging form of enterprise derives not only from algorithms of finance but also the social sciences and humanities. Key topics are the history of business, case studies of leadership in context, and debates between competing theories of how organizations function and how societies manage innovation and change. Students need the insights of psychology, sociology, anthropology, and humanities fields such as history, politics, literature, and ethics in order to develop the disciplined perspective they will need as future business persons who can grasp their shifting responsibilities and be prepared to respond quickly to new contexts. And insights from many arts and sciences fields have to be brought into productive relationship with the established business disciplines. That is unlikely to happen unless business schools come to appreciate the power of these insights for helping managers deal with the complexity and ambiguity of today's business challenges.

Awareness of this complexity is reflected in some of the teaching and learning practices we describe earlier in this chapter. Although it is deeply competitive, business education is not focused entirely on individual performance. Just as firms have to emphasize cooperation and such nonmarket virtues as loyalty in order to perform well, business programs include experience with cooperation and teamwork through their extensive use of team projects and other collaborative assignments. These forms of teaching and learning bring classroom knowledge and actual business activity closer together than is typical of most undergraduate education.

Additionally, team-based pedagogies mitigate to some degree the otherwise relentless focus on market behavior. Because effective teams need mutual trust, fairness, and loyalty, they become moral communities, even if only temporarily. To be sure, teams are formed to pursue particular purposes, and these are determined by the context and rules of the situation, whether in a course or in a firm. Some teams are focused on applying technical skills to maximize immediate profits. In other cases, team projects are designed to help students develop self-understanding, a larger sense of purpose, and an understanding of the complexities of actual management practice and business's effects on other sectors of society. With this broader framing of educational goals, team-based experiences can help to mitigate a narrow, self-enclosed perspective on the roles and responsibilities of business.

Overall, business students and faculty put their faith in active, entrepreneurial virtues, which are often seen as constituting *professionalism*—a term of moral evaluation encompassing a character ideal and style of behavior. In this view, a professional person, like a professional performance, is prepared, serious, and strategically effective, aware of and able to position oneself, one's organization, or one's cause advantageously in what is assumed to be a relentlessly competitive environment.

We would argue for a broader definition of the professional, one we discovered in only a few business programs but which is central in fields like medicine and law. The true professional embodies the field's defining purpose of service to patients, clients, and society at large. In medicine and the law, these commitments give rise to tensions and conflicts in professional practice. However, these tensions and conflicts can be a pedagogical opportunity because they open the door for students to begin thinking through the practical and moral complexities entailed in that profession.

By contrast, in business programs, attention to professionalism seldom leads students to critical reflection about the demands of their future occupational identity. The dominance of the idealized market works to erase in principle any tension between such larger purposes of business and the strategic imperative of pursuing one's own self-interest. To be sure, few faculty or students, when asked directly, affirmed such a pure version of agency theory, but they often found it hard to articulate an alternative understanding of business. This suggests that undergraduate business education is doing too little to promote intellectual curiosity or clarity beyond the boundaries of professionalism as being effective and successful within a fairly narrow conception of the field.

Preparation for Twenty-First-Century Life

In the aggregate, the result of undergraduate business education is the formation of graduates who, despite their virtues of hard work and seriousness, manifest weak understanding of, and even weaker concern for, the larger society in which they will function. The business major typically provides students with few tools or incentives to develop competence in the arts and sciences, areas that are sure to become increasingly important for business professionals.

There are two main deficits. The first concerns graduates' understanding of and attitudes toward the complexity and ambiguity they will encounter in managing knowledge and personnel, the key internal resources of their companies. The second is their capacity to understand and responsibly engage with the challenges that come along with business's growing interdependence with other institutional sectors and realms of society.

It seems clear that in the present century business will be ever more involved with government, the media, education, and civil society at all levels, often across many different national cultures and institutional contexts. Especially in light of recent challenges to the assumption that current business models will continue to spread within a global market dominated by American finance, business leadership would seem to require more, rather than less, understanding of the larger context within which business must operate. A more intentional and thorough effort to provide business students with experience moving between the perspectives of business and other sectors of society would enhance students' understanding of the inescapable pluralism of modern life. It would also serve as a stimulus toward integrative thinking, which is a critical resource in a business career. Fostering the intellectual engagement of business majors is not a distraction from their professional training. On the contrary, under today's conditions, it is fast becoming a necessity if they are to engage effectively with their vocations as business professionals.

○

With its historic commitment to combining vocational preparation with the culturally broadening effects of education in the arts and sciences, we believe American higher education is well positioned to educate for exceptional business leadership. Our examination of the actual, on-the-ground practice of education for business—which is to say the experience of business students—suggests that this ideal has not yet been achieved. But we remain convinced that, conceived in this broader way, business programs can provide the clarity and direction their graduates will need to manage the growing complexities of business life.

In Chapter Four we describe how the goals and practices of liberal learning might be reconceived—and given greater emphasis in undergraduate business programs—to better blend business and the arts and sciences in the service of a more complete and effective preparation for twenty-first-century business and citizenship.

4

THE MEANING
AND RELEVANCE OF
LIBERAL EDUCATION

IN OUR VISITS TO BUSINESS SCHOOLS, we were struck by the degree to which undergraduate business students take what they and others call an *instrumental approach* to their studies. In keeping with this mind-set, every course is judged by its apparent value as a means toward academic and, eventually, career success. For many business students, arts and sciences courses fall short by this criterion. To be sure, some business majors see college as an exciting time for intellectual exploration but more often they view liberal arts and sciences courses primarily as requirements to get out of the way.

This tendency toward an instrumental approach to education is, in part, built into the curriculum and the advising system, as we described in Chapter Three. That is, curricular programs that make explicit connections between liberal learning and business are relatively rare and student advising doesn't bring the value of liberal learning to students' attention in compelling ways. Although we saw some programs that treat business as a point of departure for engaging with issues that are especially salient in the twenty-first century, such as environmental sustainability or the effects of technology, these programs are clearly not the norm.

Few business deans or faculty, it should be said, endorse the separation between instrumental and exploratory approaches to college learning. On the contrary, most are strong supporters of educating toward a complex and pluralistic understanding of the world and want their students to experience perspectives other than business. They want to give their students the best possible education and they believe this includes the liberal arts and sciences.

Signals are mixed on the degree to which business leaders outside of academe believe this is true. A number of reports have pointed out that upper-level managers often endorse the value of a broad, liberal education (Hart Research Associates, 2010). They seem to appreciate that a larger perspective will be a valuable resource for business success as well as for life more generally. But middle-level hiring officers tend to choose candidates for skills that will be of immediate use to the company. The discrepancy may reflect not only a difference in point of view among business leaders in different roles but also a tension between what is needed for long-term success versus what is needed in a practical sense in the short term. This same tension or ambivalence about the relative value of long-term versus short-term goals is evident within U.S. business more generally.

Within higher education, it is probably safe to say that most faculty agree that education should aim to liberate individuals from unreflective conformity and help them learn to think for themselves. They believe that, above all, higher learning should promote critical thinking (DeAngelo, Hurtado, Pryor, Kelly, Santos, & Korn, 2009). But there is less consensus about what college should be freeing its students *for*. The instrumental stance, similar to the view of many companies' hiring officers, takes higher education as training to get on in life. From this standpoint, higher education stops short, or should stop short, of trying to influence the kinds of persons graduates will become. To do so would be presumptuous because it would impose values on students.

By contrast, the tradition of liberal education has generally understood freedom not as a given but as a goal that individuals must actively seek. In this view, freedom requires becoming a certain sort of person: aware of oneself as occupying a particular position in the world, loyal to particular relationships and values, but aware that there are others that need to be understood and engaged. In this view, helping students develop reflective self-awareness is a defining goal of higher education. And because self-awareness is understood to be the necessary basis for the development of genuine freedom, it has moral as well as cognitive dimensions.

As we have argued, taking part in any education program is likely to exert a shaping influence on students' sense of themselves and their potentials. Despite the inevitability of formation, though, it is common for educators to avoid or deny responsibility for education's formative effects. This happens when the college experience is marketed as simply a package of information and tools that can be picked up and used in any way the consumer wishes. But the college experience inevitably shapes the outlook and sensibility of students as well as, ultimately, their sense of who they are and what matters in their choices. Especially when business programs are coherent and consistent, they provide powerful formative experiences even if they don't address students' character intentionally or directly.

Liberal arts requirements might seem to temper or balance the instrumental stance toward education that is so widespread among business students but conventional distribution requirements offer only a weak corrective at best. General education in the form of distribution requirements is not well designed to address systematically the objectives that university bulletins and mission statements claim: the ability to bring together intellectual, cultural, and moral resources in order to solve unscripted problems; to connect knowledge across different domains and areas of experience; to imagine the world in more complex ways; and to take up a responsible position in life. Although sometimes grandiose in their formulation, goals like these are in fact realistic descriptions of the capacities that have become important in order to function responsibly in the business environment and the twenty-first-century world. The educational problem lies in the gap between aim and achievement.

In this chapter, we suggest that *liberal education's purpose is to enable students to make sense of the world and their place in it, preparing them to use knowledge and skills as means toward responsible engagement with the life of their times.* To meet this purpose, liberal education requires academic content knowledge and several kinds of cognitive skills as well as the capacity to bring this knowledge and skill to bear on complex and ambiguous issues in the real world. In what follows, we will first explain how we think these goals relate to students' need to prepare themselves for work in fields such as business. Then, taking the example of an educational experience that integrates the perspective of business knowledge with liberal learning, we will sketch the common features of this kind of education. Our aim is to provide a useful set of categories that describe liberal learning, which we will then employ in later chapters as a framework for thinking about how to improve business education by infusing it with the central dimensions of liberal learning.

The Problem: Joining Liberal and Professional Education

Business programs share with other fields of professional education the need for synthetic approaches to learning. Students in medicine, law, engineering, nursing, teaching, and other professions need to master the formal knowledge that undergirds their fields. But this is not enough. Professional programs must also ensure that their students learn how to bring that knowledge together with practical skills in pursuit of the field's defining purposes. Aspiring professionals need to learn how to draw on their knowledge and skill as they make judgments in particular situations. They must become agile in pulling together multiple sources of knowledge and points of view as they work with others to define and solve problems, learn how and when to intervene with a patient or client, and understand how to act in a challenging situation so that they uphold the best traditions of professional competence and integrity. Professional preparation must provide the experiences and the reflection on those experiences to enable students to make the best possible decision in that particular time, place, and circumstance.

Professional education uses varied pedagogical vehicles to support the development of these capacities, which are encompassed in the notion of Practical Reasoning. They range, as we have seen in Chapter Three, from case studies to simulations of practice to guided responsibility in actual practice. Through all these methods, the challenge for students is to bring together the knowledge, skills, and dispositions appropriate to the profession in flexible, integrated ways. This means being able to quickly grasp the important aspects of their clients' or patients' situations, interpret them in light of the profession's distinctive base of knowledge, and then reach a judgment about the best course of intervention for the well-being of those they are attempting to serve. This capacity to bring general, expert knowledge to bear in a particular situation is what makes Practical Reasoning central to all professional training.

Practical Reasoning

Unlike purely technical judgment, which uses well-defined methods to achieve predetermined ends, Practical Reasoning involves joining formal knowledge with the concrete and value-laden dimensions of professional practice. The pedagogies of professional education, then, necessarily involve a moral dimension: they teach students what the profession stands for and they reflect and reinforce the profession's highest standards of practice. As such, professional education is unapologetically formative, with public responsibility in view.

Whether or not business is taken to be a true "profession," professional education provides a useful analogy to the kind of educational experience that will give structure and significance to business students' learning. Like other undergraduates, business majors need to learn a good deal but they also need to learn how to *use* that learning to inform their judgment in complex situations. They need educational experiences that spur them to shape their own lives for critical engagement with their future careers. These aims converge with those of liberal education, which aspires to give students the knowledge and formative experiences they will need to gain an understanding of the world and the ability to take conscious responsibility for themselves and their lives in light of this knowledge. To achieve these aims, liberal learning needs to be concerned with developing students' Practical Reasoning.

This kind of integrated approach to learning speaks to a paradox that perplexes many individuals and institutions today. On the one hand, specialization in academic fields is similar to the division of labor that underlies economic growth: by focusing on a single goal it is possible to do progressively better at attaining it. On the other hand, decisions in professional practice, and in life more generally, often cannot be broken down into single-goal issues and require the capacity to connect, integrate, and adapt.

This is true of business as well as other institutional sectors in contemporary society. As the economic crisis of 2008 has made painfully clear, even organizations that thought they could minimize the need for Practical Reasoning—which is to say professional judgments in complex and morally ambiguous circumstances—by operating entirely according to formula have discovered, and the public has been reminded, that in the end they need people who can think about more than single-criterion efficiency. They must be able to consider and interact with a variety of interested parties or stakeholders and concern themselves with the good of the larger society as well as their own. In short, business needs personnel who are adept at thinking in an integrated, responsible way. Concretely, then, what would such an integrated approach look like? Are there models that could be drawn on to develop such an approach and adapt it to a variety of business programs? The answer is yes.

Integration in Action

In our visits to business programs, we were able to observe integrated approaches in action and in later chapters we will present a number of these. Here we will use the senior capstone experience required of all students at the Stern School of Business at New York University to clarify the salient features of these integrative approaches. Titled Professional Responsibility and Leadership (PRL), this course draws together most of the elements of liberal learning that we believe are important for business students and does so in a way that genuinely integrates the perspectives of the arts and sciences disciplines with those of business. Using this course as our starting point, we will articulate and examine the principles that underlie our aim to produce a more general model of liberal learning for students considering careers in business.

Professional Responsibility and Leadership completes a sequence of four courses that the Stern School requires of all its students. The sequence is called the Social Impact Core and it focuses on how business shapes and affects the world in order to ensure that students are thoughtful about their ability to influence society as business leaders (Stern Business School, 2010). This core sequence is one of three sets of requirements at Stern. The others are People, Information, and Systems, which includes the study of information systems and management, and Money and Markets, which comprise the required accounting, finance, and marketing courses. So, by the time students arrive in Professional Responsibility and Leadership, they have studied the four business disciplines and information technology applications as well as economics and other subjects in the university's Liberal Arts Core and electives outside business. Additionally, there is a strong theme of global awareness and the value of study abroad running throughout the curriculum. Thus, PRL is a true capstone. It explicitly draws on both the core business disciplines and a range of arts and sciences fields while focusing on issues that students will confront as professional business people in a global world and, ultimately, as leaders in business and society.

The many sections of the course follow a common syllabus developed by a team of instructors over nearly a decade. As Bruce Buchanan, the lead instructor, explained to us during our visit, the course is structured around a series of topics that range across the issues encompassed by the experience of business leadership, and the basic pedagogy for addressing those issues is discussion and writing, making it more like a liberal arts seminar than a typical course in the business disciplines. The class discussions engage students in lively exchange about case studies drawn from actual business experience, which are then complemented by readings from a wide variety of fields, including business theory, history, literature, psychology, and ethics.

Although students prepare background readings in advance, they are often presented with cases only on arrival in class. This, says Buchanan, is "to mimic how things like this crop up unexpectedly in professional life. . . . These are treated like real-time cases. We try to resolve the case in the class session." The cases, then, are used to simulate actual situations, enabling the seniors to practice the ability to analyze and discuss problems on the spot, working like a management team. Students are asked to make use of their knowledge of the business disciplines and techniques for problem solving and they are also asked to relate their responses to the background readings in liberal arts disciplines. This promotes a complex process of back-and-forth cross-referencing between the situation into which the case plunges the students and the literary, historical, or philosophical texts and contexts they have been exploring. Students are also given considerable writing experience and feedback on their writing. In the course section we observed, for instance, students do journal entries guided by the instructor's understanding of the larger, integrative aims of the course. "We're trying to get the students to think for themselves," Buchanan explained. "In writing the journals, they need to say what's on their minds, to begin a conversation with themselves." Stern students are often "so focused they have no time to reflect on what they really want to do . . . this makes them stop and think . . . in a very safe way."

The importance of time and space for reflection comes in part from the demographics of business students at NYU. The students are very strong academically, especially in quantitative abilities. A significant number are first-generation college students, many foreign-born, and often under pressure from their families to succeed professionally above all else. Many are there because, as we were told, they know that "NYU feeds Wall Street." Given this context, the Social Impact Core, and especially the capstone course, aims to help these students develop the conceptual vocabulary for thinking about their careers in relation to their developing goals and identities as persons. The object of the writing assignments, in particular, is to provide students with new resources and conceptual tools for thinking about their lives and future possibilities within the broad horizon of business in society.

One strategy that Professional Responsibility and Leadership uses to help students think about their goals and directions is to present, especially through the cases, as much of the full complexity of actual business life as possible. Students are asked to enter imaginatively into a variety of business contexts, from large financial organizations to small, entrepreneurial firms to major corporations to consulting businesses. The intent is to provide opportunities to imagine working in these alternative settings and to recognize what is and is not valued in each while exploring how the circumstances represented in the cases fit or challenge the students' own beliefs and purposes. Another strategy is to use the readings including fiction and other narrative literature as a way to develop insight and gain conceptual resources for dealing with the major ethical challenges of business. The syllabus provides various, sometimes surprising, perspectives that students can discuss and employ in making sense of the problems with which the cases confront them class by class.

For example, students encounter cases that depict conflicts between the individual's apparent, immediate advantage and his or her commitment to an ethic of responsibility as employee, employer, or citizen. The complementary reading is from the Roman advocate and statesman Cicero, who wrote a short philosophical work for his son entitled *On Duties*. Interestingly, Cicero uses cases drawn from the life of his times to lead his son to explore the kinds of moral conflicts to which active involvement in business or politics gives rise. The guiding question Cicero poses is how to reconcile opportunities for one's own advancement or enrichment with a commitment to ethical integrity, equity, and the moral priority of the common good. Perhaps not surprisingly, many of the students in Professional Responsibility and Leadership find themselves mirrored in the text, both personally and professionally. Even when they challenge the text and despite (or perhaps because of) its distance in time and cultural context, students discover that they can use it as a resource for imaginatively thinking through the implications of the contemporary challenges presented by the cases at hand.

By engaging with such classic readings, this course enables students to go beyond merely stating and arguing their personal opinions. Instead, they discover that their own questions have a history and can be better understood when placed within the larger context of critical arguments that make up an intellectual tradition, such as moral philosophy in the case of Cicero's *On Duties*. They see that having access to the past enriches and gives depth and perspective to present circumstances. And, in the Social Impact Core, that past is increasingly a global one that draws on the cultural heritage of several traditions.

But the intellectual resources of the humanities and social sciences employed in the course are not introduced simply for their own sake as objects of connoisseurship. Instead, they provide scaffolding and context within which the students can better learn to think for themselves, an important goal of the course. In a word, the course tries to persuade students to take *striving for wisdom* as a serious goal. The cases and readings, the discussions, and the journal entries are all means toward enabling students to confront with competence and poise the endemic tensions they will have to negotiate as business professionals.

Professional is, in fact, arguably the operative word in this course. Whereas technicians might construe their function as simply making things go more efficiently, improving the means without caring about the ends, Professional Responsibility and Leadership emphasizes business as a profession rather than simply a set of morally neutral techniques. Business, in other words, is understood as a potentially humanizing vocation that commits its practitioners, as all professions do, to serve certain ideal values and social benefit. The PRL capstone draws on the technical knowledge students have acquired as well as ideas from beyond the business context in order to provoke students to reflect on their own struggle for integrity. It holds out challenges and models of ways to balance personal opportunity with societal well-being, technical innovation with ecological stability.

By any standards the course is well conceived and executed and it stands out for its use of pedagogies and perspectives that are unusual in business programs but characteristic of teaching and learning in the liberal arts and sciences. The strength of the Stern School's approach to integration is that liberal arts perspectives are brought to bear on concerns that immediately engage the students: career questions but also issues about who they wish to become and how they want to live. This is liberal education, then, but with an edge. As another instructor told us: along with teaching practices and concepts drawn from the arts and sciences, the Stern program adds the dimension of Practical Reasoning—having to make and consider judgments of value and decisions for action—to intensify and focus the classic liberal arts and sciences pedagogies.

Liberal Learning's Three Modes of Thought

If Practical Reasoning is a kind of synthetic capacity, entailing the integration of a range of knowledge, skills, and dispositions and manifest in decisions and actions, liberal learning can be seen as a way of thinking about the world. It has, certainly, been defined by many thoughtful observers and advocates over the years; our conception, drawing on the history and tradition of liberal education (Association of American Colleges and Universities, 2005; Nussbaum, 1997; Orrill, 1997; Schneider & Shoenberg, 1998) focuses on three major modes of thought, which we term *Analytical Thinking, Multiple Framing,* and the *Reflective Exploration of Meaning,* along with Practical Reasoning (see following page). These modes of thought provide a framework for our integrated vision of liberal and business education. To highlight their importance, we capitalize them throughout this book.

Liberal Learning and Its Central Dimensions

The purpose of liberal learning is to enable students to make sense of the world and their place in it, preparing them to use knowledge and skills as a means to engage responsibly with the life of their times.

Analytical Thinking

Analytical Thinking abstracts from particular experience in order to produce formal knowledge that is general in nature and independent of any particular context. It is methodical and consistent, beginning with a particular set of assumptions or categories and proceeding to develop the implications of these concepts through deduction. Examples of such discourses range from mathematics and logic through theories in various disciplines such as economics.

Multiple Framing

Multiple Framing is the ability to work intellectually with fundamentally different, sometimes mutually incompatible, analytical perspectives. It involves conscious awareness that any particular scheme of Analytical Thinking or intellectual discipline frames experience in particular ways.

The Reflective Exploration of Meaning

The Reflective Exploration of Meaning encompasses the most self-reflective aspects of learning. It involves the exploration of meaning, value, and commitment. It raises questions such as what difference does a particular understanding or approach to things make to who I am, how I engage the world, and what it is reasonable for me to imagine and hope. This is the traditional heart of liberal education, the focal point of humanistic learning.

Practical Reasoning

Practical Reasoning represents the capacity to draw on knowledge and intellectual skills to engage concretely with the world. Practical Reasoning allows the individual to go beyond reflection to deliberate and decide on the best course of action within a particular situation. Such thinking is characteristic of professional judgment, including that of business leaders, as well as being a key capacity of citizens and statesmen.

Analytical Thinking

This mode of thought is the most basic and pervasive feature of higher education. It corresponds roughly with what developmental psychologists call *higher-order thinking* and to what is commonly understood as *conceptual* or *abstract thinking*. It is found in virtually every college course and is in many ways the coin of the realm: you can't get anywhere without it. It consists of two closely related operations.

The first is classifying a concrete event, fact, or phenomenon within some universal category so that the particular comes to be understood as an instance or a case of *x*. In this way, Analytical Thinking translates concrete experience into abstract propositions. The second feature of Analytical Thinking consists of manipulating these categorized particulars according to general rules or principles, for instance, when students learn in algebra to apply general rules to solve equations for the particular values of variables.

In every form of Analytical Thinking, particular aspects of experience are categorized according to some scheme of general concepts and then operated on by formal rules of transformation. This is often described as logic and is best illustrated by mathematics but it is also present in the sciences and in the verbal analysis of concepts and arguments. Together, these two intellectual operations—categorizing concepts and operating on them according to rules of procedure—stand at the core of rigor as it is understood in the academy. Since the 1959 Ford and Carnegie Corporation reports on undergraduate business education, which criticized business programs for their lack of analytical rigor, this kind of thinking has become a fundamental goal of business programs—and of faculty seeking academic legitimacy.

Accordingly, analysis is typically the key condition that must be met for a course or program to be considered academic in nature. This is why, as various practical and professional endeavors have entered the university, they have uniformly set about producing theories of their practice expressed in conceptual or theoretical terms. Analytical Thinking, then, corresponds to those aspects of business thinking that are essentially matters of technical mastery (Martin, 2007).

Teaching for such thinking provides practice in classifying a set of ideas or phenomena and bringing these under formal rules of operation. (Plane geometry has long been thought of as a kind of primer for this kind of thought.) But an exclusive focus on this kind of learning, although it strengthens students' mastery of important technical reasoning tools, is also inherently limiting. Such teaching does not promote the questioning of assumptions; rather, it postulates or defines and then develops a single point of view and way of thinking. The aim is to operate *with* the concepts, not to question or think *about* them. Although this is arguably necessary in order to gain proficiency in the use of problem-solving tools, the preponderance of such experiences in undergraduate business education creates an atmosphere in which the critical understanding of concepts is pushed to the margins of the curriculum. For students immersed in the analytical mode, then—whether in business, engineering, or the sciences—concepts that concern interpretations of the *meaning* of experience, as in the disciplines of history, philosophy, literature, and the arts, are not likely to seem rigorous or even perhaps properly academic.

Because learning the technical disciplines at the heart of the business curriculum demands the repeated practice of distancing—of the concepts from particular instances and the modes of thinking from personal experience—it is easy to overlook the deeply formative influence of such education. However, as we have seen, any repeated activity that requires intensity of concentration, such as that demanded by the technical fields in business, shapes attitudes and dispositions. By necessity, students become highly invested in the types of intellectual activity that constitute the specific field of study—and in the personal attitudes and dispositions these investments of self demand. There are parallels here to the education of students in technical fields such as engineering (see the research by Gary Downey on engineering courses in Sullivan & Rosin, 2008, pp. 47–56). In other words, the formative effect of the typical business curriculum is to reinforce the idea that real knowledge is formal knowledge accessed by Analytical Thinking and as such requires no personal interpretation—and can even demand its suppression.

The roots of these attitudes may well antedate the students' arrival in a business program, reflecting differences in interest between students who develop a strong inclination toward making things work compared to students more at home thinking imaginatively and in reference to personal identity and social interaction. These differences have been noted for decades and are familiar to many as what psychologist Liam Hudson (1966) characterized as convergent versus divergent thinkers. The former are typified by business (and engineering) students who are facile in finding answers that converge as closely as possible to a fixed outcome. By contrast, the divergent thinker is inclined toward open-ended questions that require imagining possibilities. There are echoes here of the instrumentalist versus explorer attitudes described by the business and arts and sciences students with whom we spoke.

The danger posed by an exclusive attention to Analytical Thinking is that it threatens to close off developing minds to the exploration of perspectives that are crucial for understanding and relating to the full scope of modern realities. Indeed, the educational challenge in business programs is to motivate convergent thinkers to develop an interest and some facility in concepts beyond the purely analytical. This is important, as we have argued in previous chapters, because in order to make sense of complexity, students must also learn to negotiate opposing and inconsistent ideas, to become aware of the contingency of particular viewpoints, and to develop cognitive skills for coping with that realization. They must, in a word, learn to work with our second mode of thought in liberal learning, Multiple Framing.

Multiple Framing

The second characteristic dimension of liberal learning is Multiple Framing, a mode of thought that enables one to perceive and deal with fundamental inconsistency and contradiction. The need for this mode becomes apparent when one confronts questions and problems whose complexity or ambiguity does not give way before the clarity and rigor of analysis. Analytical Thinking is inadequate in such situations not only because the sheer degree of complexity can sometimes overwhelm one's analytic capacities, but also because some kinds of ambiguity or subjectivity are inherent in the problems and questions themselves.

For some kinds of problems, there are several frames through which one might make sense of the issues, each of which makes different starting assumptions and therefore appropriately takes different considerations into account. Practically speaking, this means that even models or systems that are internally coherent and make sense analytically, given their starting assumptions, may not be the only or best way of framing a problem. And Analytical Thinking cannot in itself resolve basic differences between competing, fundamentally different models or theoretical perspectives. Teaching Multiple Framing involves helping students learn that any particular way of framing the issues is contingent in some sense and they should come to recognize the nature of that contingency—in relation to history, culture, ideology, and the like.

We refer in previous chapters to research showing that outstanding business leaders excel at being able to hold several, often conflicting, viewpoints in mind so as to derive a new, integrated understanding. Because these leaders are aware that particular approaches to a problem are just that—particular and organized from a single point of view—they are able to see that any given way of framing issues is not necessarily the only or best way to do so. They understand that frameworks and definitions of problems are created by people, not given in the nature of reality (Martin, 2007). A dose of healthy relativism about fundamentally different approaches to problems, then, is an intellectual virtue that business professionals need to cultivate. The mode of thinking we call Multiple Framing allows them to do just that. When students learn Multiple Framing, they come to recognize that different approaches, with their particular categories and assumptions, illuminate aspects of problems that other approaches do not; they learn that in order to solve complex problems it is necessary to look at issues from several, not always compatible, points of view.

For example, students in the Stern School's Social Responsibility and Leadership course come to see that a purely financial approach to an issue could miss things that an organizational behavior perspective reveals and that both approaches could, in turn, be blind to ethical issues that appear from the perspective of communities affected by the issue. This capacity to shift frames gives students a wider range of conceptual tools they can apply to a situation without becoming overwhelmed at the apparent messiness produced by conflicting assumptions about what should guide business decision making. Multiple Framing is critical to these students' ability to negotiate the pluralistic social contexts in which business actually functions.

Traditionally, in the liberal arts, Multiple Framing has been called dialectical thinking. In courses in rhetoric and writing, for example, Multiple Framing or dialectical thinking is employed in the familiar pattern of compare-and-contrast reasoning. This kind of practice is valuable training for business professionals because it underlines the importance of point of view and thus the realization that any analytical approach is always one among many. As students come to see that they are always operating from their own point of view, or to realize that they in fact *have* a viewpoint through which they are experiencing reality, they also discover that theirs is only one among many possible perspectives. Recognizing that one has a viewpoint is thus a portal to understanding the nature of *argument*: the comparison, contrast, and judgment of competing viewpoints. This is the essential point and key method of Multiple Framing.

Additionally, the discovery of viewpoint and the capacity for Multiple Framing changes the student's perspective on the significance of Analytical Thinking. No longer an end in itself, Analytic Thinking now appears as a tool or means for taking part in argument, a way to advance and weigh evidence or claims about a particular understanding of the world. Clearly, students need both modes of thought.

The Reflective Exploration of Meaning

A third mode of thought is needed as well. Analytical Thinking and Multiple Framing have limitations (separately and even together) that demand that they not be the exclusive focus of teaching and learning in undergraduate programs. The former prizes analytical skill in solving convergent problems and this strength is also a limitation, just as a too-narrow focus on market thinking can restrict the judgment of business leaders. The difficulty with Multiple Framing as a mode of thought is its tendency to produce intellectual fatigue, skepticism, and even cynicism. Arguing both sides of every issue can lead students to think that "it's all relative" and that therefore all opinions have equal merit. For some students, this may even seem to justify using immediate self-interest as their primary decision-making criterion. In the context of these limitations, our third mode of thinking, the Reflective Exploration of Meaning, provides a counterpoint, explicitly taking up questions of orientation and purpose, and providing solid grounding for choice, direction, and commitment.

The Reflective Exploration of Meaning is the mode of thought that encompasses the most self-reflective aspects of learning. Analytical Thinking demands evidence and rigor and Multiple Framing asks about the strengths and limitations of methods of investigation and frames of reference. This third mode pursues a deeper, more self-reflective question: what difference does a particular understanding or approach make to who I am, how I engage the world, and what it is reasonable for me to imagine and hope? As such, it helps learners confront uncertainty amid conflicting understandings to arrive at commitment to purposes adopted with reflective awareness. The Reflective Exploration of Meaning is therefore of crucial importance to today's business students and in fact to all undergraduates.

In particular, as a mode of thought concerned with questions of meaning, value, and commitment, this third mode within liberal learning lies at the heart of *interpretation*. And though interpretation takes different forms in different contexts, certain features of interpretive reflection are common across many disciplines and settings, suggesting a four-part taxonomy of this third mode.

NARRATIVE. The first of these features is that the Reflective Exploration of Meaning is often *narrative* in form. It is "thinking through story." Such thinking places the reader vicariously in the action, exciting the imagination and inducing the reader (or listener) to assume one or more positions in relation to others and to specific contexts. This feature of narrative is familiar to everyone; engagement with narrative entails imaginative participation in the experiences being described. It is by imagining the stance of others that reflection on narrative stirs new insights along with a greater awareness of one's own stance, something that, until that time, may have remained wholly unconscious. In business courses, the appeal of using cases and so-called war stories of business practice reflects the pedagogical power of this first feature of the Reflective Exploration of Meaning.

QUESTIONING. The second feature concerns the questions that seem to arise spontaneously when reading or discussing stories. Who is this character, for example, and how does she feel about this other character or event? What is this character hoping for, afraid of, trying to do, and so on? What values define that character's stance toward the world and toward others? These questions are often the substance of business cases as well as the pedagogy of literary and historical analysis. They ask readers to abstract certain features from the narrative, seeing them as instances of more general categories in order to gain an explicit understanding of aspects of the characters, action, or situation—a process that brings Analytical Thinking to narrative. This pedagogy of questions also makes possible a variety of other cognitive activities, including the use of Multiple Framing to gain insight by comparisons among points of view.

PRESENTATION. In classes where the instructor—or the instructor's questioning of students—breaks apart a text under discussion, students are typically asked to imitate these processes orally or in writing. This is the third feature of the Reflective Exploration of Meaning: learning to interpret texts by presenting an analysis of their significance in public. Within professional education, this feature of the reading and interpretation of texts has its direct analogue in the presentation of cases and reveals the essentially communicative or rhetorical nature of the practice of interpretation. In fully formative teaching, this sequence of activities—the vicarious engagement in narrative, questioning and critical analysis of the narrative, and the presentation of an interpretation of the significance of the narrative—is repeated, often in increasingly complex forms, so that the practice of critically reading texts becomes familiar enough in its out-lines to become the object of intentional practice and development on the part of the student. Feedback is a crucial aspect of this process, as well, taking the form of response by peers or by the instructor (and better yet, by both) on the spot or in later written feedback.

APPLICATION. Finally, the Reflective Exploration of Meaning entails a process of application. Here the key questions are what does this char-acter, situation, or narrative mean for me? How should it affect my sense of how things are, of who I am? What does it ask of me and how should I respond? This process leads naturally to Practical Reasoning, as described earlier in this chapter—the reflective decision to act in a certain way in light of one's sense of purpose given the particular circumstances of the present. In well-designed educational experiences, students draw on all three modes of liberal learning as they engage problems and situ-ations that demand Practical Reasoning.

Returning, then, to the Stern School's Social Impact capstone course, Professional Responsibility and Leadership, we see that it relies on nar-rative, both in using cases as prompts to student involvement and in many of its assigned readings, especially those drawn from history and literature. The discussion and writing assignments ask students to inter-pret the problem the class is confronting that day in light of the texts under consideration and also encourages them to draw on their own experience. Students are thereby using both Analytical Thinking and Multiple Framing. Throughout, the course asks students to analyze cases and readings, sifting and evaluating alternative framings of the problem and its solution along various dimensions of value: monetary, strategic, communicational, and ethical. And they do this publicly through discus-sion and presentation. As they repeat these practices of interpretation, the students carry on a dialogue with their classmates and the instructor about the significance of the cases. As they write, reflecting on the rele-vance of the readings for understanding the cases and their implications for action, the students are also, as Buchanan told us during our visit, developing a dialogue with themselves about how they intend to act as business professionals and who they wish to become. By having to resolve together each day's case-based business problem, students are being given repeated, mentored practice in Practical Reasoning, which integrates all their other thinking. This process exemplifies what we mean by the integration of business education with liberal arts and sciences content through Practical Reasoning.

Opening Up Reflective Space

Although we see Practical Reasoning as crucial to our conception of liberal learning, the liberal arts and sciences disciplines tend, ironically, to be weak in addressing this goal. Professional fields do much better. Professional fields such as law, medicine, architecture, and engineering prepare their members by emphasizing the formal, universal concepts that undergird their fields, but they also go beyond theoretical learning and teach their students how to relate this learning to the demands of particular clients, patients, and technical or social problems. Often this is done through the use of case studies, simulations, and guided participation in and reflection on actual professional practice, strategies that are sometimes (but not frequently enough, we would argue) employed in the arts and sciences. Earlier, and in subsequent chapters as well, we examine several examples in business programs in order to suggest what is possible.

It is equally important to emphasize that, although a judgment about particular problems of practice must serve technical and pragmatic ends, in order for it to count as *good* professional judgment, it cannot be entirely instrumental. That is, professional judgment must not only be guided by rich knowledge and strong technical skills, it must also be aligned with the public purposes, ethical principles, and ideals of the profession. Teaching judgment thus requires Practical Reasoning, which brings together the three modes of thinking by integrating them into a particular resolution for which students must then take responsibility. This engagement with responsible decision making provides a new, richer starting point for the students' further development as professionals and educated, integrative thinkers.

When reflection on personal and moral significance is organically linked with Practical Reasoning, the organizing aim is, in essence, *practical wisdom*. This phrase captures the multifaceted expertise embodied in wise, capable, and thoughtful practice. Preparation for every profession ought to be concerned with how to improve its students' commitment to this goal. But especially for those who are concerned with the social meaning and contribution of business, the cultivation of Practical Reasoning that aims for wisdom should be understood as essential.

○

From the outset of our study, we made the assumption that undergraduate business students can experience the key modes of liberal learning described in these pages through courses in the business curriculum and through other experiences within their business education as well as in arts and sciences courses. Neither taken alone is sufficient. If students gain the full array of Analytical Reasoning, Multiple Framing, Reflective Exploration of Meaning, and Practical Reasoning entirely within arts and sciences disciplines, they will almost certainly have difficulty translating that understanding to their preparation for business. If they gain experience with these dimensions of liberal learning exclusively within a business context, their college experience will be impoverished and they are unlikely to graduate with a deep understanding of the world and their place in it. For that, a good deal of what is traditionally understood to be liberal arts and sciences content is needed as well.

The two content areas are therefore interdependent and must be coordinated. In the best examples we encountered, they are. Further, students need intentional, institutional support in actively connecting liberal learning with learning that is directed specifically toward preparation for business careers. In our selection of site visit campuses, we looked for programs that are self-conscious about ensuring that their students receive a strong liberal education and that have mechanisms in place to help students integrate their business and liberal learning. In the next several chapters, we look more closely at some of these efforts and will draw out principles that can be of use elsewhere.

5

TEACHING FOR
KEY DIMENSIONS OF
LIBERAL LEARNING

EARLIER IN THIS BOOK, we argued that undergraduate business majors benefit from an expanded understanding of business in which they come to appreciate the relationship of markets and economic systems to other social institutions and forces. We have tried to show why students need a well-developed capacity to deal with ambiguity or uncertainty and a firm grasp of relevant knowledge they can draw on when facing challenging situations. We believe that liberal learning, properly understood, can contribute to these outcomes through the inculcation of the three modes of thinking described in Chapter Four, the content needed for students to make sense of the world and their place in it, and the capacity to bring all of these together in wise Practical Reasoning.

This conception of liberal learning captures a number of educational priorities or goals that apply to all undergraduates, including business majors. However, articulating these learning outcomes is one thing; teaching for them is yet another—and easier said than done. The goal of this chapter is to describe more concretely what it means to teach for Analytical Thinking, Multiple Framing, the Reflective Exploration of Meaning, and Practical Reasoning, sampling different approaches to each. In doing so, we hope to show how students can gain the essentials of liberal learning both in their business courses and in courses originating from the liberal arts and sciences disciplines. As emphasized throughout this book, both are necessary if undergraduate business students are to be well prepared for responsible work, engaged citizenship, and satisfying personal lives.

Teaching for Analytical Thinking

Though the terminology may vary, the kinds of outcomes captured in our notion of Analytical Thinking are universally endorsed by faculty and administrative leaders throughout higher education, who place it at the top of their list of goals for student learning (DeAngelo et al., 2009). This emphasis reflects the fact that Analytical Thinking lies at the heart of scientific inquiry and the technological innovations that flow from it. It is a crucial skill for democratic citizenship as well and the basis of rational discourse in every domain.

As we discuss in Chapter Four, Analytical Thinking involves the formulation and rigorous application of abstract concepts. It requires students to understand particular events as instances of more general concepts and to learn how to formulate claims and make valid arguments using those concepts. Analytical Thinking pertains to operations that are quite simple and also to those that are extremely complex and sophisticated. It makes sense, therefore, that these capacities are stressed *throughout* undergraduate education, within both the arts and sciences and business curricula.

Analytical Thinking is taught in many arts and sciences disciplines, especially the sciences, mathematics, philosophy, economics, and other fields in which rigorous logical analysis plays a central role. It is also an important goal within the business curriculum. Introductory courses in accounting, which are required for undergraduate business students regardless of their specialization, illustrate the teaching of Analytical Thinking in the context of technical systems within a particular business function. In this way, basic accounting courses reveal an approach that is an integral part of many undergraduate business courses.

An Example from Introductory Accounting

We saw many well-taught introductory accounting courses that address Analytical Thinking, including an excellent one taught by Virginia Soybel at Babson College. Like other accounting courses, this one concentrates on helping students learn systems for representing various kinds of financial information and provides an overview of the role of financial information in economic decision making. In doing so, it works back and forth between examples of real data—balance sheets from actual companies, for example—and various abstract representations of those data. In the class we observed, Soybel helped students work their way through the logic of three alternative systems for representing the cost of goods sold by a company. These three systems are called first in, first out (FIFO); last in, first out (LIFO); and weighted average. And though our purpose here is not a lesson in accounting, it is worth taking a moment to explain the meaning of these terms for readers who are not familiar with them.

Under FIFO, the cost of goods sold is based on the cost of materials bought earliest in the period. With LIFO, goods sold are valued based on the cost of material bought at the end of the period to be represented. The remaining inventory (unsold goods) will correspondingly be valued based on materials bought earlier under LIFO and later under FIFO. The weighted average approach values both the cost of goods sold and the remaining inventory based on the average cost of all units available for sale during the reporting period.

The financial implications for the company of these different accounting systems vary depending on several factors, including economic trends in the period in question. So, for example, during periods of inflation, the use of FIFO will result in the lowest estimate of the cost of goods sold and therefore the highest net income for the company. Likewise, the use of LIFO will result in the highest estimate of the cost of goods sold and thus the lowest net income. There are reciprocal implications for the valuation of inventory, which is represented as an asset on the company's books.

In order to understand the logic of these accounting formulas, students need to work their way through them step by step. Soybel helps them do this by demonstrating the application of the three methods to several data sets and then requiring students to work out, through class discussion, the reasons that companies might prefer to use one or another of these systems under particular kinds of circumstances—asking them, for example, to explain the tax implications of the three methods during a time of inflation. In the course of the discussion, Soybel frequently references how actual companies choose to report such matters, interweaving information, such as legal requirements, that provides a context for the discussion.

The abstract nature of these representations is underscored by Soybel's reminder to students that "when we're talking about financial accounting, it doesn't necessarily represent the physical flow of goods." When a student makes a comment that confuses the physical flow with the accounting of goods, Soybel takes the opportunity to clarify the distinction. Although the difference between physical flow and accounting flow underscores the abstract nature of analytical concepts, this does not mean that teaching Analytical Thinking relies entirely on abstractions.

In fact, working through concrete examples in a step-by-step manner is essential for gaining facility with the concepts and logical principles that form the basis of this mode of thought.

Soybel's course also illustrates how Analytical Thinking can be used to generate a list of advantages and disadvantages of different systems of calculation under different conditions and is, therefore, an important contributor to decision making. Of course calculating outcomes under different scenarios from within an analytical system is not, in itself, sufficient for making a decision about what technique to use; decisions about how much priority to place on minimizing tax liabilities (to cite just one example) relative to other, competing goals take one into the realm of Practical Reasoning. But Analytical Thinking provides critical information for that kind of integrated decision making.

More Complex Contexts

Some applications of Analytical Thinking are relatively simple, such as those illustrated by Soybel's class session from introductory accounting. But this mode of thought can also be employed in relation to problems of significant complexity when there are multiple factors to account for and many individual and interactive effects to reason through. This is evident, for example, in more advanced contexts such as the finance course we observed at the University of Pennsylvania's Wharton School. This course addresses international, monetary, and financial economics and aims to provide a framework for analyzing macroeconomic events such as business cycles and long-term economic growth.

Discussions of complex issues of this sort dramatize how important it is for Analytical Thinking skills to be well honed; the greater the complexity, the greater the need for powerful conceptual models that direct data selection and assessment, and for rigorous thinking in working through the logic of complex systems. Given where most college students start, it is difficult for undergraduates to achieve highly sophisticated levels of Analytical Thinking. It is useful, therefore, to teach for Analytical Thinking in connection with many different content areas to give students extended and varied practice with this mode of thinking throughout their undergraduate years. The ultimate goal is to provide essential analytical tools for dealing with ambiguity, allowing the analyst to identify a multitude of intersecting factors and to begin to describe how they interact to produce particular outcomes.

The importance of sophisticated Analytical Thinking is vividly illustrated by the financial situation that came to a crisis in 2008 when the public began to hear about financial derivatives using collateralized debt obligations and credit default swaps (for example, McDonald & Robinson, 2009; Sorkin, 2009). As these complicated instruments evolved to become yet more complex and intricate, even sophisticated technicians in the financial industry had trouble gauging their value. This situation dramatizes the need for advanced Analytical Thinking and also reveals its limits. A clearer understanding of these and other complex financial innovations would have made their risks more evident but judgments about how much risk to accept cannot be decided solely on the basis of analysis.

Teaching for Multiple Framing

Research on cognitive development has shown that most students come to college believing that there are right and wrong answers to every question, even if the right answers are not yet known even to authorities. Questions that require judgment and that allow for multiple solutions are, therefore, especially confusing to students at first. Over time, however, they develop a greater awareness of the inevitable uncertainty or subjectivity of some kinds of questions and a recognition that there may be many strong solutions (and, for that matter, an essentially endless number of weak solutions) (King & Kitchener, 1994).

That is, as students learn and develop intellectually, they come to see that for some kinds of problems there is more than one interesting, productive, and persuasive way to frame the issues, and that fundamentally different approaches to that framing are sometimes equally compelling from an analytical perspective. The capacity to apply several different interpretive frames to a set of observations and to make a strong case for each one is, in fact, a hallmark of liberal learning. As someone once quipped, a liberally educated person can analyze Freud from a Marxian perspective and Marx from a Freudian perspective. This observation acknowledges that theoretical frameworks emerge from particular historical, political, cultural, and intellectual contexts. The more students are able to understand ideas as contextually rooted, the broader, richer, and more sophisticated their thinking will be. The need for this kind of Multiple Framing in advanced intellectual work makes it clear that Analytical Thinking, as powerful as it is, does not provide all of the intellectual tools needed to negotiate today's complex world.

The arts and sciences faculty we spoke to in our site visits often stressed the importance of helping students appreciate and negotiate ambiguity. Their comments reinforce the importance of the intellectual capacities entailed in Multiple Framing. Students must learn to call into question assumptions that they had previously taken for granted and to see that beginning with different starting assumptions often leads to dramatically different interpretations with potentially divergent implications for how one operates in the world.

As we describe in Chapter Three, teaching students to question assumptions is not a particular strength of undergraduate business education. Typically, students are asked to learn and apply standard business concepts without considering their origins and broader significance. When concepts are taught in this way, students tend to see them as corresponding to some objective reality instead of as tools created by human beings. This problem is exacerbated when individuals remain embedded in a single conceptual frame over an extended period of time (as the dominance of the efficient market model in business almost ensures), coming to treat the model as real even if they are aware on some level that it is not. This tendency, which philosophers refer to as the *reification* of abstract ideas, makes it difficult to know what to do when confronted with opposing but equally compelling perspectives. (The term *reification* derives from the Latin *res*, meaning *thing*, so literally reification refers to making abstract concepts into concrete things.) Business faculty may contribute to reification but they can also counteract it. When, for instance, students are asked to apply alternative frames to phenomena of interest, they not only gain intellectual sophistication about the nature of concepts and models, but they also learn substantively about the historical, cultural, and political roots of powerful models and other theoretical assumptions. Understanding that "it hasn't always been this way" and that "not everyone sees it this way" frees students to think more creatively, potentially supporting innovative reframings that greatly strengthen their ability to negotiate the complex realities of the contemporary world.

In our campus visits, we saw a number of missed opportunities to introduce Multiple Framing. In a class on business operations, for example, students were learning to define and calculate "process cycle time" (the capacity of the slowest stage in the process or the stage with the lowest output) and "throughput time" (the sum of times for each step in the process). The lecture and the questions posed to students focused on how to use this information to increase the efficiency of any process. This teaching strategy seemed to be effective in helping students understand and use the concepts. But an additional benefit might have followed if students had been asked to address the concepts' central assumption—that maximizing process efficiency is an overriding goal of business operations—or to the associated concept of workers being much like machines. The lesson might have been strengthened as well by discussion of the historical roots of the assumptions underlying these contemporary business concepts (for instance, from Frederick Taylor's management science theory, which courses in management often treat as outmoded in contemporary business). Clearly, these kinds of pedagogical moves don't just happen; teaching for Multiple Framing is a challenge.

Fortunately, we were lucky enough to see several examples of purposeful attention to this mode of thinking. In fact, some programs make a point of combining the teaching of Analytical Thinking and Multiple Framing into a single integrated experience, both early and late in the undergraduate experience.

Multiple Framing in a Course on Economic Perspectives

Franklin & Marshall College, for example, offers a course available to all students and popular among those interested in business. Introduction to Economic Perspectives introduces multiple perspectives on economic theory early in students' college careers. It meets in a freshman residence hall and the professor, David Brennan, stresses the value of broadening students' perspectives at this early stage instead of "inculcating a single perspective [in this case neoclassical economics] over and over until their thinking becomes so narrow that they have lost the interest or even the capacity to entertain other frames for understanding the discipline." Toward this end, the course examines a set of topics about which students generally have a lively interest—for instance, labor markets, business organizations as institutions, prices and values, business cycles and instability, and the environment—considering each from the perspectives of several economic theories. This topical rather than strictly theoretical approach helps students understand why these differences in perspective matter. Often, students read essays based in mainstream neoclassical assumptions and go on to a series of critiques of or alternatives to those assumptions. A central goal is to legitimize for students ideas outside the consensus view of neoclassical economics that dominates many business schools and departments. Clearly, this course teaches Analytical Thinking as students learn to trace through the implications of each theoretical perspective, but it also teaches Multiple Framing as they consider several alternative ways to make sense of the same basic phenomena.

In the class session we observed, the topic was timely: theoretical perspectives on the nature and causes of the then-ongoing economic crisis of

2008. The discussion pulled together and explored the major explanations given for economic stability and instability in neoclassical, Keynesian, and Marxian theories. Lively discussion linked the theoretical explorations with the unfolding world economic crisis, asking questions such as whether economic systems are inherently stable or unstable and why. The range of answers illustrated, in turn, fundamental differences among the three theoretical perspectives. If markets are assumed to be self-regulating, sources of instability must be exogenous. If markets are not self-regulating, stability depends on a variety of policy tools—for example, raising the marginal propensity to consume or invest by various tax and fiscal policy means. If capitalism is inherently unstable, as in Marxian theory, why is that and what kinds of cycles would this perspective predict?

Among other things, Brennan asked the class to consider "why we should continue to study Marxian perspectives today" when they have little remaining political influence. He pointed to the descriptive usefulness of a dialectical model in which high growth is followed by crisis, which then leads through instability to a new configuration, which begins yet another cycle of growth. Even if one does not accept Marxian theory more broadly, Brennan told us, "this account provides some perspective on what is happening now that isn't available within the neoclassical perspective, which assumes a smooth growth curve unless exogenous shocks intervene."

In considering this course on economic theory, it is important to note that at Franklin & Marshall economics is a discipline within the arts and sciences, though it is also an essential component of undergraduate business training. Constructing the course to consider the implications of major economic theories rather than solely to develop technical expertise is a very "liberal arts kind of approach." And this is not an accident, because the college's Business, Organizations, and Society program is designed to teach business from the perspective of liberal learning.

To say that Brennan's is a "liberal arts kind of approach" may, however, invite a misunderstanding, suggesting that such courses are of only impractical "academic" interest. The opposite is true. Helping students broaden their perspectives is a way of preparing them to confront a range of difficult questions they will encounter in the world of business and beyond, worlds where they will be challenged time and again to negotiate ambiguity without oversimplifying complex issues. In order to ensure that students are well prepared to do this, Franklin & Marshall's Business, Organizations, and Society curriculum teaches the skills and mind-set of

Multiple Framing throughout students' undergraduate years, treating this outcome as a defining characteristic of the major.

The need to foster the capacity for Multiple Framing as well as Analytical Thinking illuminates the essential role of the traditional liberal arts and sciences for broadening the perspectives of business students. Seeing beyond conventional frames and imagining multiple, even irreconcilable conceptions of phenomena require students to draw on broad knowledge from a range of disciplines. Substantive content is involved because imagination requires more than logic and more than abstractions. For this reason, students need to engage with liberal learning content in their business courses; they need to take courses in liberal arts and sciences disciplines and receive support and guidance to connect what they learn in those settings with what they learn in business courses.

Historical Thinking as Multiple Framing

For example, history courses and historical themes within courses in other disciplines provide fertile occasions for students to practice Multiple Framing as well as Analytical Thinking. Central goals of the discipline of history are to devise fresh explanations for historical events, to formulate and defend interpretations, and to sift, assess, and offer evidence— all essential elements of Analytical Thinking. But the study of history also teaches students to understand events and issues within the context of their particular time and place. When historical thinking is applied to phenomena central to the world of business, students come to see that the status quo they take for granted does not represent an enduring reality. These phenomena are evolving and a grasp of their historical roots often changes how their present form is understood.

During our visit to Indiana University's Liberal Arts and Management Program (LAMP), we observed courses that illustrate the constructive use of historical thinking for broadening the perspectives of students preparing for careers in business. One of the LAMP seminars, called The Automobile: Economy, Politics, and Culture, takes an explicitly historical perspective. Through consideration of the history of the automobile in America, this seminar ranges across topics such as the early years of the automobile industry as a representation of "the genius of the American business system," the automobile as a promise of liberation during the progressive movement (1870–1920), sex and the automobile in the jazz age, gender relations in the mid-twentieth-century automobile industry, the suburbanization of the United States, and more. Especially in light of the current crisis in the American automobile industry, a sense of the trajectory of that industry in the context of social, political, and economic history is particularly enriching to students' understanding of the relationship of business to other social forces.

Teaching for the Reflective Exploration of Meaning

The capacity to consider and manipulate multiple frames greatly enhances students' intellectual power, enabling them to imagine alternative ways to think about important issues and to grasp the historical, ideological, and cultural contingency of any particular interpretation. As we discuss in Chapter Four, this increased appreciation of varied interpretations and perspectives is essential for students in any field of study and can make a dramatic difference both intellectually and practically for students who are preparing for careers in business. But unless this rigorous thinking is directed toward some committed purpose, it can lead to relativism or cynicism—or at least to a narrowly instrumental orientation.

A strong education in Analytical Thinking and Multiple Framing without attention to meaning can teach students to formulate and critique arguments, but this very facility can make it hard for them to find any firm place to stand. For this reason, Analytical Thinking and Multiple Framing need to be grounded in and guided by the third mode of thought in liberal learning—the Reflective Exploration of Meaning, which engages students with questions such as "What do I really believe in, what kind of person do I want to be, what kind of world do I want to live in, and what kind of contribution can I make to that world?" Lack of attention to this third mode is a dangerous limitation, especially when students are preparing for work that has important implications for the welfare of society.

More Than Ethics

Ethical considerations are clearly central to this third mode but the Reflective Exploration of Meaning is not reducible to ethics in any conventional understanding of that term. In fact, many courses in moral philosophy are notable for their exclusive focus on Analytical Thinking and Multiple Framing. By contrast, the Reflective Exploration of Meaning explicitly encourages and provides guidance for students to engage with questions of personal meaning, value, and commitment. This requires the capacity to imagine multiple versions of the good life and to explore the meaning of those visions for one's own guiding ideals, moral identity, and life purpose. In this sense, self-exploration, identity, and self-understanding are essential features of the third mode. Especially when this exploration is disciplined and enriched by skilled analysis and an awareness of multiple frames, it can broaden one's identifications and loyalties and embed within the self a commitment to social contribution.

To be clear: just because a course addresses topics of values or ethics, it does not follow that the course connects these topics with students' efforts to make personal sense of the issues or to explore the meaning *for them*. This point is illustrated by a course called Moral Problems and the Good Life, offered as an elective at one of our site visit schools. With that title, one might expect that this course would involve students in thinking through the implications of various conceptions of the good life for their own identities and commitments, giving them a sense of where the meaning and purpose of their lives might reside. Instead, this course offers a stimulating and rigorous philosophic treatment of issues such as hedonism, intrinsic and extrinsic or instrumental value, the nature of the moral community, and the character and extent of human beings' obligations to each other.

Each class session in this course considers arguments made by philosophers who have written about the issue under consideration along with analyses and critiques of and counterproposals to those perspectives offered by other philosophers. The course's substantive topics are surely of significant personal interest to students and its scholarly sophistication and intellectual rigor is exceptional, especially at the undergraduate level. These are excellent means of developing students' intellectual capacities and knowledge and could constitute a strong foundation for the subsequent exploration of personal meaning in relation to important issues. But in its existing form, the course does not ask students to think about the meaning and purpose of their own lives. This may happen for some students, certainly, but the course does not pursue such a goal directly or explicitly.

Some of the other courses we observed *do* address this goal, however. Consider, for example, a course called The Philosophy of Work, offered in the philosophy department at Bentley University. Taught by Carolyn Magid, the course begins by asking students to reflect on their own work experiences, thinking about what they want and need from work. It then moves to consider a range of ethical issues in the contemporary work world, addressing such topics as globalization, workers' rights, and gender equity in the context of ethical theory and scholarship. The course draws on a range of texts and other materials from literature, history, philosophy, and public policy, requiring students to think analytically and dialectically using multiple frames. But woven throughout is a thread that connects each set of considerations to students' own beliefs about the issues discussed, to explorations of their commitments and values, and to the personal meaning of work for them.

Professional Responsibility and Leadership

We also saw courses *within* the business curriculum that teach the Reflective Exploration of Meaning. We describe one of these in Chapter Four: Professional Responsibility and Leadership, a required course for seniors at NYU's Stern School of Business. This course asks students to consider the role of business in society, the economic and ethical aspects of acting as a business professional, and the relationship of these topics to the creation of a meaningful life. Course materials include readings and cases from business practice as well as an extensive set of liberal arts classics by authors such as Anton Chekhov, Walt Whitman, Confucius, Plato, Cicero, and Machiavelli. In drawing on this wide array of literature, professor Bruce Buchanan wants to show students that moral wisdom can be found in many disciplines, from many parts of the curriculum, not just in moral philosophy courses.

As Buchanan described it to us, Professional Responsibility and Leadership aims to get students to *think*—to understand what their professional options are and how to make thoughtful, well-informed choices about their futures in business, to recognize that their choices will affect the meaning of their lives and the kinds of people they become, and to have a conceptual vocabulary for thinking and talking about ethical issues and choices. "They're choosing a firm and an industry and need to understand what they will be called upon to do. They need to think about how that relates to what kind of person they will become," Buchanan told us. He helps students think about the significance of wealth and its relationship with other goods, human rights as well as legal rights in a global context, and the kinds of ethical issues that come up often in business, such as conflicts of loyalties and interest, responsibilities in situations of information asymmetry, and so on.

Throughout the course, Buchanan makes it clear to students that they need to take ethical responsibility for their own behavior, no matter what their superiors call on them to do. "There is a lot going on in industry that is questionable, and they need to be able to recognize that something is amiss as soon as possible and to understand where their true long-term best interests lie. . . . They need to be aware that the system is not always honest. I make an effort to be hopeful and positive but also put them in a position to make better decisions." He suggests that students need to consider the degree to which they may compartmentalize the different areas of their lives and end up playing a role that they need to distance themselves from, raising the question of whether there is an authentic moral self at the core of their various roles.

Teaching for Practical Reasoning

Practical Reasoning, as we explain in Chapter Four, involves using all three modes of thought along with theoretical concepts, knowledge, and skills and guided by values and commitments, to function effectively in the world of practice. The cultivation of Practical Reasoning enables students to move between the distanced, external stance of Analytical Thinking—the third-person point of view—and the first- and second-person points of view from which one must act when solving problems with others in real situations. This involves moving back and forth between general concepts and the particular challenges and responsibilities that come with each unique situation. Teaching for Practical Reasoning thus prepares students to use knowledge and skills to engage with complex problems, formulate judgments, and take action in situations that often involve considerable uncertainty.

In life after college, students will need to draw on their knowledge and intellectual skills as they think through and resolve practical issues. Yet it is unusual for undergraduates to gain significant practice using what they have learned. This is an area in which professional and vocational education can provide leadership for the arts and sciences, which place even less emphasis on teaching for Practical Reasoning than do the professions.

One might think that students would need to gain significant knowledge and skill first and then learn how to apply those resources in the context of practice. But, in fact, courses that centrally address Practical Reasoning and the integration of theoretical and practical understanding can provide a great deal of new knowledge as well as support the integration of knowledge and skills learned previously. As we discuss in Chapter Three, Babson College provides an intriguing example of teaching for Practical Reasoning. The business curriculum there immerses all freshmen in an intense, full-year course that requires them to start and run small businesses at the very outset of their college years. Foundations of Management and Entrepreneurship (FME) is meant in part to level the playing field, putting students who have not yet worked in business on a more equal footing with the many Babson students who have already taken part in starting or running businesses when they arrive at college.

FME pairs interactive lectures with the experience of developing and screening ideas for a business in the first semester and starting a select subset of those businesses in the second semester. In the process, students put systems in place for many business functions, including market research, inventory management, accounting, performance appraisals, e-commerce, and customer relationship management. In this way, the course fosters very real technical skills as well as substantive knowledge and interpersonal capacities. Because all students experience this course in their first year at Babson, faculty teaching upper division courses can count on students having had a significant business experience in which to apply new learning.

A major goal of this course—at the heart of our vision of liberal learning for business education—is that students experience business as an integrative enterprise; starting and running a business makes the interconnected nature of business functions very real for students. Each student is part of a functional department in the new company so the team may hear from the sales people, for instance, that the marketing department does not have an effective strategy. The marketing staff may then point out that it does not have the budget for a more ambitious approach. Students in the finance department explain that the revenue is insufficient because sales are low. Team meetings give students in all departments an overview of the issues, which makes it clear to them that each part of the business depends on the others and that, when the company is not flourishing, systems and their inter-relationships need to be improved on many fronts.

FME addresses the full array of business disciplines (finance, marketing, management, accounting, human resources, operations, information technology, and communications) and students are highly motivated to learn because they have an immediate need for the knowledge and skills. They also achieve a more grounded understanding of the concepts through their application. In-class simulations help make abstract ideas real even before students attempt to apply those ideas in their businesses.

The class we observed began with a fast-paced, hour-long segment that moved from lecture to discussion to simulation. Then the class turned to reports by student teams on the businesses they were running. Professor Steve Gordon and his teaching partner grilled the presenters mercilessly, holding them accountable for both process and outcomes. In connection with the disappointing sales figures of one team, for example, the discussion touched on whether to revise sales projections and, if so, how much and how to decide. The discussion moved next to the question of quotas for members of the sales team. In the course of that discussion, Gordon took the opportunity to explain the differences in the use of sales quotas in different types of businesses, ultimately suggesting that this team establish process rather than outcome quotas. "It would be better to put quotas on something you can control, such as the number of sales contacts each team member makes."

Each company engages in 360-degree performance appraisals, which require students to evaluate themselves, their peers, those who report directly to them, and managers. Based on these evaluations, students receive a comprehensive report on how they are perceived by others. This is just one of many ways that students receive ongoing feedback on their work. When students are struggling, faculty members schedule supplemental class sessions, use peer mentors, add extra office hours, and give additional exercises. The idea is to ensure that all students achieve the goals of this demanding course. In the process, they learn about the critical importance of drive and persistence, working hard and seeing the results of that investment pay off, and being part of a team that works well together. As Gordon told us, "I'm teaching, critiquing, lifting morale, teaching how to be a citizen of the world, how to be responsible not just to themselves, but also to the team and the business."

This account of FME illustrates the fact that Practical Reasoning is inherently integrative. It draws on Analytical Thinking, Multiple Framing, substantive knowledge, and the craftsmanship of professional skills. Further, if Practical Reasoning is going to result in wise professional judgment in the fullest sense, it must be guided by a strong sense of social purpose and responsibility, a well-developed sensitivity to ethical issues embedded in the complexity and ambiguities of real situations, and experience coordinating and resolving potentially conflicting claims and perspectives. It must also build on and be guided by the third mode of liberal learning, the Reflective Exploration of Meaning. Of course, undergraduate education can make only a start on the life-long development of mature judgment and expertise. But the college experience is a powerful one and it can establish trajectories that go on to make an important difference in the years after graduation.

A Capstone Example

In order to achieve a broader sense of professional formation, professor of management Gregory Baker weaves a thread of ethical and social or public policy considerations throughout the capstone business strategy course he teaches at Santa Clara University. The course teaches the concepts and methods of strategic management, providing hands-on experience and connecting business strategy with the exploration of personal and company values and corporate social responsibility. The course is taught from the perspective of the general manager, who is responsible for the long-term prosperity of the organization. A major part of the course involves presentation and discussion of Harvard Business School cases, and students write case analyses both individually and in teams. These write-ups include analyses of markets, critical success factors, competitors, and major social, political, economic, and technological factors that present threats to or opportunities for the industry.

Prior to the class session that we observed, students studied a case about a large genetic engineering company based in the San Francisco Bay Area, not far from the Santa Clara campus. The case raises questions about business strategy for this company, which produces pharmaceuticals. As they engaged with the case, students imagined that they were advising senior management, senior scientists, or the board of directors with regard to three key functional areas—finance, marketing, and production. As Baker introduced the discussion, he noted, "The important thing is to ask the right questions and lay out the right alternatives. The answers will flow from that."

Implicit in the discussion was an image of business as competitive, fast moving, always changing, involving a lot of risk, and requiring smart thinking to minimize that risk and maximize profit. In order to succeed under such conditions, one must be constantly working out effective strategies on multiple fronts. The class mimicked this process by working intensively to identify key issues, determining how to choose among various strategies for addressing the issues, and deciding what considerations should be taken into account in light of the complexity of relationships among the various issues.

Baker emphasized to students that often the most obvious approach to a problem does not turn out to be the best approach. Students grappled with this when talking about production issues, for example. They began the discussion of production by suggesting that the pharmaceutical company ought to organize itself to produce as much product as possible at the lowest cost. But Baker's pointed questions and comments led students to recognize that this is only one possible strategy within a wider array of options. "Don't assume that because this is a pharmaceutical company, it has to immediately become a 'fully integrated' pharmaceutical company," he noted. Other options include licensing the technology, selling it, contracting with another company for manufacture or distribution, or creating joint ventures with larger pharmaceutical companies. In reality, the company in question chose to partner with its biggest competitor in a joint venture, an approach the students had not thought to consider.

Despite the emphasis on profit-making strategies in a competitive market, Baker also found seamless ways to introduce ethical issues throughout the conversation. For example, at one point the group was talking about the importance of protecting research and development investments with patents, so Baker took the opportunity to talk in greater depth about the nature and implications of patents. The conversation focused on intellectual property rights, the complex relationship of patents to the public interest, and related issues. In a typical question during this conversation, Baker asked, "Who are the stakeholders and who are the beneficiaries of patents?" This question led to a rich discussion of both positive and negative consequences to the public from patenting scientific discoveries.

Later, during a discussion of the company's need for top scientists as employees, a student returned to the intellectual property issue, pointing out that many scientists prefer not to work for profit-making companies: "In science, people have to publish their work and make it available to the field, because science depends on people being able to build on each others' work." Another student picked up on this remark, commenting, "My father is a scientist and he used to work for a profit-making company but left because of ethical concerns."

In a conversation after class, we asked Baker whether he believes that financial success in a competitive market is the overriding goal of business. His answer was predictably nuanced: "I do think our system is based around a contractual agreement between businesses and stockholders that management will make maximizing economic value the central goal," he said. "But I also try to make students aware that that is not the only way it can be done." He does this, he says, mostly by contrasting the American system with those of other countries that take a somewhat different approach, with the American approach being "the most capitalistic capitalist system." This comment nicely represents the teaching of Multiple Framing, with the implication that students also need to explore for themselves the meaning of the assumptions embedded in the different frames.

Meeting Multiple Challenges

When students major in business or some other professional or vocational field, it is clear (in a way it sometimes is not in the arts and sciences) that college must impart knowledge and skills in ways that make them usable in the world after college—certainly for the graduates' work but also for their lives as citizens and as thoughtful and responsible individuals. If this is the aim, it is clear that undergraduate education requires the integration of learning across developmental dimensions and across subject matter specialties. Yet each domain of learning presents its own challenges. Few students come to college with well-developed capacities on any of the four dimensions of liberal learning. During the undergraduate years, students must learn to think both clearly and broadly, to explore the direction of their lives, and to use knowledge to solve complex problems in the world.

One key challenge is to teach toward abstract intellectual capacities, to make concepts real, and yet at the same time to make students aware that these *are* concepts, not reality itself. If Analytical Thinking is emphasized to the exclusion of other modes of thought, concepts and models may become all too real for students. That is, students may reify conceptual frames, mistaking these abstract representations of reality for reality itself. Pedagogical strategies are needed that help students understand that concepts are tools human beings create to simplify and represent symbolically the features of reality that play key roles in particular theoretical formulations.

But even advanced intellectual virtuosity that includes the capacity for Multiple Framing is not sufficient as preparation for work and for life. Intellectual rigor and facility must be strongly grounded in the human purposes that rationality and rigor are meant to serve. So the integration of learning must also include the exploration of meaning and purpose, shaped and informed by knowledge and clarity of thought.

○

In our fieldwork, we saw imbalances in emphasis among the essential learning outcomes of undergraduate education and we saw missed opportunities to expand learning to include the full range of outcomes. This was true in arts and sciences courses just as in business. Yet we also saw compelling examples of creative teaching that addresses intellectual processes, substantive knowledge, personal meaning and direction, and Practical Reasoning in both the arts and sciences and the business curriculum.

We have described here some courses that stand out as supporting learning in this full sense. In Chapter Six, we will take a closer look at some pedagogical strategies that are especially valuable in achieving these outcomes.

6

PEDAGOGIES OF LIBERAL LEARNING IN BUSINESS EDUCATION

UNDERGRADUATE BUSINESS STUDENTS need a strong liberal education in which they grasp abstract ideas and understand the implications of those ideas for the complex situations they will confront in work and life. They need powerful analytical skills and well-developed historical and cultural perspectives to inform the way they perceive, understand, and solve problems. They need the capacity to step outside taken-for-granted assumptions and narrow framings to recast issues in fresh and productive ways. They need to achieve at least a provisional sense of direction and meaning, to reflect in a disciplined and informed way on their life choices, and to develop commitments consistent with their examined values and convictions. And their professional and personal judgment should be informed by insights into themselves and others as well as an understanding of and commitment to the ethical standards and social significance of their professional roles. These liberal learning outcomes are essential if students are to move from narrow technical expertise to professional judgment and responsibility.

None of these outcomes can be achieved without involving students actively in the learning process. As illustrated by the courses featured in Chapter Five, this means engaging students in a diverse array of assignments, including team-based activities, business-case analyses, simulations, and practice with oral presentations and written communication. And because the goals of undergraduate business education are best understood as broad and varied, instructors need to be able to draw on a variety of instructional approaches. In particular, students need a hearty dose of pedagogies that entail active engagement. In this way, choices faculty make about *how* to teach are at least as important to student learning as *what* is taught. Indeed the two cannot be separated; desired learning outcomes must be matched with appropriate pedagogies.

How are instructors to align teaching with desired learning outcomes? The basic principle is simple: *teach students what you want them to know and be able to do.* Unfortunately, this principle is easy to invoke, often hard to enact, and rarely pursued in an intentional way in course or program design. To ensure that students understand an idea deeply, it is important for them to practice the tasks that constitute and reveal understanding as shown by explaining the idea in their own words, representing it in new ways, applying it in new situations, and connecting it with practical contexts. But often students are asked to practice distant substitutes for what faculty really want them to know and be able to do. Those substitutes are more likely to be selected based on academic tradition and ease of delivery than on intentional matching of teaching strategies with learning goals.

In aligning teaching with learning goals, it is critical to recognize the central place of *purposeful practice* in the development of expertise. Effective teaching for any kind of expertise or competence requires the instructor to demonstrate or model the skill or capacity, provide opportunities for students to practice the demonstrated elements of competent performance, and provide corrective feedback on students' performance along with an explanation of that feedback. Typically, multiple cycles through this practice-feedback sequence are required. In this chapter, we examine a range of pedagogies that promote this kind of deep learning.

Teaching for Expertise

Following Grossman, Hammerness, and McDonald (2009) and Grossman and McDonald (2008), we use the term *pedagogies of enactment* to refer to approaches that are explicit and intentional about representing expertise and providing practice accompanied by informative feedback. These pedagogies require students to perform or *enact* their skills and understanding in extended, supervised practice. This category intersects with the more familiar set called *pedagogies of engagement* (see, for example, Smith, Sheppard, Johnson, & Johnson, 2005), which are active learning or student-centered pedagogies designed to engage students more deeply than lectures typically do. They also often connect students with the local community. Thus, pedagogies of engagement include problem-based learning, service learning, learning communities, and undergraduate research. What we have called *pedagogies of enactment* represent a subset or variation of the broader category, with a special focus on involving students in extended supervised practice of the desired skills and elements of understanding. In this sense, the two categories are not coextensive, though both are important to business education, and promising examples of both are featured in several previous chapters.

The profile of these pedagogies of enactment is distinctive within the business major—differing from approaches used in other vocational fields and in the arts and sciences disciplines. These distinctive pedagogies, including the use of teamwork, cases, and simulations, are often deeply engaging for students. When executed skillfully, they offer powerful learning experiences. But it is helpful to look critically at the limitations and risks as well as the benefits of these teaching strategies (see Chapter Three), thinking about how to strengthen them by expanding the range of outcomes they support and aligning them more firmly and fully with desired outcomes.

Teamwork

Unlike most undergraduate majors, contemporary business education makes extensive use of team-based pedagogies. Business programs at the undergraduate and MBA levels began increasing their attention to teamwork as a pedagogical approach in the 1980s, at least in part in response to employers who were dissatisfied with the ability of recent graduates to work successfully in teams. Tom Ehrlich, when he was president of Indiana University, regularly heard this view expressed by business executives at the Business–Higher Education Forum, an association of leaders from educational and business realms.

It now appears that educators are responding vigorously to this message. We saw pedagogies involving teamwork in business courses at every campus we visited and at every level from the freshman to the senior year. Although teamwork is employed throughout the curriculum, it is particularly prevalent in integrative courses and experiences, such as the introductory business course, activities designed to integrate the core business disciplines, and senior capstones. The freshman year Foundations of Management and Entrepreneurship course at Babson College, discussed previously in this book, illustrates how participation in teams representing varied business functions helps students experience the interdependence of different departments in working businesses and thus supports their efforts to bring together what they are learning in different business disciplines.

Interestingly, the activities that students carry out in teams—research projects, case analyses, presentations, and so forth—are usually not very different from the kinds of assignments they do individually. Likewise, the content knowledge addressed in the team's work may be exactly the same. What, then, does teamwork add? One answer is that peer collaboration, including simply studying in groups, is well known to facilitate learning (Light, 2001). When students have to explain challenging ideas and other course material to their peers, and when they need to reach agreement on how to use the knowledge conveyed in the course, they are *practicing their understanding*—putting ideas into their own words, drawing out the implications, explaining the logic of an argument to a critical audience, and so on. It is no wonder, then, that students learn more course content when collaborating with others than when studying on their own. Teams naturally draw out the cycles of practice and feedback that characterize effective pedagogies of enactment.

In addition to facilitating the mastery of content knowledge and intellectual skills, working together in teams can also enable students to practice skills they would not otherwise exercise. These include many of the capacities required to apply what they are learning to complex, real-world problems through Practical Reasoning: creating shared goals and strategies, allocating tasks efficiently and fairly, persuading their teammates to adopt particular goals or approaches, engaging differing perspectives with civility and respect, negotiating compromise solutions to disagreements, managing conflict and other difficult group dynamics, and motivating others to do their part. When students work with teams that are diverse in the skills and knowledge members bring to the group or in cultural or social class background, they often remark on how much they learn about ways to cooperate across differences in order to work together productively.

Teamwork can also help students develop personal qualities that are important for success, such as reliability, time management, flexibility, tolerance, and open-mindedness. In the highly competitive environments of many business programs, it can be especially beneficial for students to learn how to control their individual ambitions and egos for the sake of the team's effectiveness. Professor Anderson Williams at Morehouse College commented, for example, that students come to his Principles of Management course with strong personalities, accustomed to doing their work alone. But he tells them that working alone is not an option in business; they need to learn to function as part of a team.

The Importance of Feedback in the Learning Cycle

A central challenge for almost every team is to learn how to handle the "free rider problem" (Ashraf, 2004), that is, how to deal with group members who do not carry their weight. Sometimes, students who are more responsible but would not ordinarily exercise leadership step forward to take the reins. In other cases, the offending group members come to see in a new way how important it is to meet their obligations and to do so on time. Faculty provide a number of tools that groups can use to manage free riders and the use of these tools is itself instructive for all involved. It is typical, for example, for grades on group projects to be based in part on peer evaluations. In some cases we observed, groups were even allowed to fire team members who were not performing adequately. One student described the trauma of being fired by his teammates and how much the experience taught him about himself and how he needs to change to become the person he wants to be.

In Leadership and Communication in Groups, a freshman course at the Wharton School, peer feedback is taken a step further. Students provide qualitative comments about themselves and their teammates and rate each team member using numerical scales. The resulting information is used by teaching assistants as they meet individually with class members to discuss how they are doing and what they could do better. Receiving this kind of frank feedback early is especially useful for setting a productive direction for the students' development during college.

Intentionality

Clearly, pedagogies that involve teamwork can be very powerful learning experiences. But fully achieving intended goals requires intentionality about the learning process—teaching students what you want them to learn. This involves making explicit the various aspects of the expertise entailed in productive teamwork, framing these outcomes for students conceptually, providing opportunities for students to practice the various elements of that expertise, and giving students feedback that is carefully designed to move them toward increasing expertise in the particular capacities needed for working together effectively. This is the pedagogies-of-enactment cycle.

We saw this kind of intentional teaching for expertise in a number of the courses and other programs we observed. Babson College's Coaching for Teamwork and Leadership (CTL) Program provides one, albeit somewhat unusual, example. In this ambitious program, coaches, who are trained alumni volunteers, conduct assessments of students' teamwork and leadership skills during the second semester of their first and third years. In these assessments, several coaches observe small teams of students working together on a case-based project. Following that activity, the coaches meet together to come to consensus about their assessments, then meet one-on-one for an hour with each student to provide individualized feedback on various dimensions of leadership including influencing others to accomplish a task, teamwork and collaboration, oral communication, listening, decision making, and ethical awareness. This kind of assessment not only provides experience and direction regarding important skills and personal qualities, but it also helps students learn how to coach their employees when they become managers, addressing employees' performances in concrete, positive, and nonjudgmental ways.

These examples stand out for their intentionality—and also because they are rare. Although we saw inspiring positive examples, our site visits revealed that this kind of intentionality about learning goals and informative feedback is often missing from team assignments. In fact, the processes and elements of teamwork may not be taught explicitly at all. Even when team assignments are prevalent, students are left to sort out on their own how to make the whole more than the sum of its parts. The results can be disappointing. For example, we saw some team projects that were little more than a series of unrelated presentations by the individual members of a team. Care is needed to be sure that students really collaborate in team projects rather than simply dividing up the work and proceeding individually. As one professor told us, "Too often, students are doing group work, not real teamwork." If this is true, it could help to explain why the undergraduate fields that use the most teamwork, business and engineering, are among the lowest reporters of outcomes such as "learning from the perspectives of others" and "coming to understand people different from the self" in national studies of college students (National Survey of Student Engagement, 2010). These are disappointing findings because it would seem that high-quality teamwork should facilitate an appreciation of perspectives that are different from one's own.

Moreover, team activities can sometimes be formative in ways that are of questionable consequence. They may, for instance, be structured as win-lose competitions. Many business students enjoy competition, which can be counted on to engage their spirited participation; taken on its own, a competitive approach to team projects is probably benign. But combined with the hegemony of market-based thinking, which infuses both the explicit and implicit business curriculum, this approach may contribute to the development of a short-term profit orientation rather than a social trusteeship model of business leadership. On a more immediate level, win-lose competitions can give the impression that business, and maybe even life more generally, is a zero-sum game. This kind of team activity misses the opportunity to foster a habit of seeking win-win solutions as the first choice in conflict situations—a strategy well known to facilitate successful negotiation (Fisher, Ury, & Patton, 1997).

Supervised Practice

Sometimes team-based activities are designed to create new small businesses, as in Babson's Foundations of Management and Entrepreneurship course. More often, students participate in supervised practice within existing businesses or organizations, either as part of a course or as a self-standing internship. This kind of supervised professional practice is commonplace in professional education, especially medicine and nursing, but is largely absent in most arts and sciences disciplines. Here again, professional programs, including business, offer valuable models and lessons for undergraduate education more broadly.

Mentored practice has many virtues. It is ideal for making abstract ideas real, for teaching students to put their growing knowledge to use, and for demonstrating and helping students experience the integrative nature of business through Practical Reasoning. Engagement with actual business practice can also foster students' personal development and, if it is given attention, their professionalism.

As with team projects, however, mentored experience alone cannot be counted on to achieve the full range of desired learning outcomes. These outcomes require intentionality in shaping the activities students pursue, in providing feedback and direction, and in structuring *productive, disciplined reflection* on those activities. Moreover, students in internships and other kinds of supervised business practice learn from what they see and do, just as in any other kind of teaching. It is worthwhile, therefore, to make a careful assessment of what experiences these programs actually provide (or don't), how students are spending their time, and then, if necessary, to make changes that align the experience more closely with desired outcomes. In our site visits, we saw courses and programs that bring this kind of intentionality to practice-based teaching and learning. Among those that do so are well-designed service-learning courses. Service learning, also called *community-based learning,* engages students in organized, sustained community service activity that is related to their classroom learning and meets identified community needs. Students then reflect on that experience, connecting the service experience with the substantive content of the course.

In these courses, students typically work with local nonprofits or small businesses to help them address real challenges they are facing. Classroom discussions and other required elements of the course provide for structured reflection on the students' practice experiences and connect those experiences with key concepts and other substantive goals of the course. For example, in the Wharton first-year course we mentioned previously, Leadership and Communication in Groups, students engage in service projects in Philadelphia to help them understand, at the outset of their business education, that business is always part of a larger social fabric and that they have obligations to help strengthen that fabric.

At Portland State University (PSU), a capstone course popular with business majors connects students with small minority- or women-owned businesses in the area. The course spans two quarters and operates through PSU's Business Outreach Program, which provides support to participating businesses. In teams of four to six, the twenty-five students in the course work on a project that they design collaboratively with the small business they are assisting and studying. The team we observed included students from accounting, marketing, management, and finance whose task was to consult with a restaurant that wanted to open a second location, helping the owners investigate and develop plans for this possible expansion. The course employs pedagogies of enactment, which include close guidance from faculty and significant structured time for reflection on and analysis of the consulting process.

Taking a somewhat different approach, Babson College's elective course Management Consulting Field Experience teaches the skills of management consulting by engaging small groups of undergraduates as consultants to nonprofit organizations under the direct supervision of MBA students. Acting as project managers, the graduate students provide detailed ongoing feedback to the undergraduates, with oversight by regular course faculty. The development of integrity and professionalism is an explicit goal, and half of the course grade is based on assessments of students' progress toward professionalism. The other half is based on the quality of the work they produce as they consult with their organizations.

Case Studies

Business education has been known for its distinctive use of case analyses and discussions. The field has long recognized that the practice of business requires more than classroom-based academic knowledge. It also requires know-how that is closer to what we have called Practical Reasoning. Business case studies, in essence, stand in for actual practice because students are asked to respond to case material "in role" as if they were preparing background material for strategic decision making, for example, or advising the company's board of directors or management. As in most real business situations, such work often involves teams. In that sense, cases, teamwork, and simulations intersect in what can sometimes be very ambitious projects.

At their most extensive, case-based projects bring together learning across several subject areas, requiring students to integrate their subject matter knowledge and bring it to bear in a practicelike situation. This is the purpose of the culminating assignment in the Kelley School of Business's semester-long integrated core curriculum (I-Core) at Indiana University. During their junior year, Kelley School students take four semester-long courses at the same time: marketing, finance, operations, and strategic management. Then, during the final two weeks of the semester, student teams act as divisional managers or consultants, advising upper management about the design of a major capital investment project involving the development of a new product. In the process, the students develop a sixty- to seventy-page case report offering a comprehensive analysis, complete with recommendations for the new product launch.

The case report has three main components. First, the teams carry out separate analyses based on each of their core classes. In the strategy assignment, for example, teams examine the strengths, weaknesses, threats, and opportunities of the company overall and the new product launch in particular. In the second component of the project, students bring together the subject-specific assignments from marketing, operations, strategy, and finance to create an integrated evaluation of the firm, including recommendations for improvement. In order to highlight the interconnected nature of business, teams must explain how changes in one part of the business are likely to affect the other parts. For the third component, teams craft an executive summary that outlines recommendations along with supporting arguments and data.

As students work through this extensive case, they become more adept at picking out the important issues embedded in a complex set of circumstances. They learn which data sources illuminate what kinds of questions and how to present the information so that it will be most informative for decision making. Overall, the process follows the formula for effective teaching that we laid out at the outset of this chapter: students are shown the expertise of strategic decision making, they practice it, they receive feedback on their efforts from both their peers and the instructor, and then they step back to ask why some approaches are better than others, and under what circumstances.

This kind of ambitious assignment is challenging and consuming for students. It provides a window into business, making classroom learning more real in ways that are seldom experienced by students in arts and sciences majors. For this reason, its formative effect on students' orientation to their future careers and their broader worldviews can be powerful.

Whether case-based projects are as extensive as this one or more circumscribed, they are most powerful when structured by the instructor to teach students what features of complex business cases are relevant for what purposes and how to find and compile the information needed to illuminate important questions connected with the case. This not only supports the development of expertise but also establishes habits of mind and characteristic ways of framing complex and ambiguous information. It directs attention to some features over others, creating a sense of salience that becomes habitual, and, eventually, even automatic and unconscious.

Case Studies and Ethical Formation

A recognition of the formative effect of case discussions underlies Santa Clara professor Gregory Baker's practice of weaving compelling ethical questions into his business strategy class's case discussions, as we describe in Chapter Five. In Baker's view, ethical concerns are part of the fabric of every strategic consideration and cannot be separated from more practical and strategic questions. Also significant from a formative perspective is Baker's insistence that his students think beyond conventional assumptions rather than automatically applying standard concepts to the case at hand. He urges his students to think, to question, and not to hesitate to make suggestions that may at first seem surprising. It is telling that Baker opened the discussion we observed by stressing that students' critical task is to ask the right questions—and only then to search for answers. This approach emphasizes flexibility of thinking, encouraging students to question assumptions and frame problems in fresh ways as well as to make effective use of standardized analytical frameworks.

If all case discussions were to include ethical considerations, these otherwise invisible issues would be more likely to stand out in students' business lives after graduation. The ability to discern the ethical questions that are embedded in complex and ambiguous situations, which the moral development field calls *ethical sensitivity*, is known to play a critical role in mature moral judgment and action (Rest, 1979). Students develop ethical sensitivity when they practice identifying the moral issues and questions raised by cases that also address practical and strategic questions. This points to the importance of integrating business ethics into broader discussions of business issues rather than routinely segregating it from the rest of learning—in special, designated ethics courses, for instance.

Even so, students do benefit from opportunities to explore their ethical responsibilities in greater depth, and case discussions can also play an important role in business ethics courses and others that provide that depth. One way to give students experience framing and managing ethical questions is to provide practice applying heuristics of various kinds to case accounts. Especially when they are understood as one of several useful ways to frame the issues, heuristics can provide at least a rudimentary sense of where to begin as students think about the kinds of difficult ethical questions that can arise in connection with their work.

Frameworks and Heuristics for Case Analysis

Consider, for instance, Joel Rubin's course on business ethics at Indiana University's Kelley School of Business, which applies a heuristic to case analysis that surfaces the many, sometimes conflicting, roles and responsibilities of managers. Rubin's semester-long course is built around fourteen in-depth case studies, each considering a different ethical issue. Students analyze each case in terms of the multiple roles and responsibilities of managers. Unlike most ethics courses, which tend to focus on classic theories in moral philosophy, Rubin's heuristic employs a scheme closer to business practice, Badaracco's "four spheres of executive responsibility" (1992). The four spheres correspond to four roles, each of which makes different moral claims on the manager: as a person, as an economic agent, as a company leader, and as a citizen thinking beyond the firm's boundaries.

In a discussion of a case about outsourcing production of AT&T's consumer electronics, for example, Badaracco's framework provides the basic categories of analysis. Rubin then begins discussion with a big question: Should companies ever outsource? Parsing the question, he leads students through a detailed discussion of the roles and responsibilities arising from the four different moral spheres, raising questions such as "What are your responsibilities to the people losing their jobs?" and "What must company leaders do to remain competitive?" Rubin wants students to learn that wise decision making involves trade-offs and must take account of short- and long-term effects and their consequences for multiple constituencies. The goal is for students to develop a habit of thinking ahead ethically, he explains, so that they "won't get into situations they don't want to be in" and will make decisions they are comfortable with and believe in.

At the end of some class discussions, Rubin asks students to role-play a scenario based on the case. Role-playing adds another dimension to learning by offering students the opportunity to practice, in the moment, how they might respond to a difficult situation. Simulating the pressures of the moment helps students reflect on their own values, beliefs, and decision-making processes as well as provides practice in responding to these kinds of situations in a safe environment. The formative power of this kind of course is evident and it underscores the value of bringing ethical considerations into case analyses, including with cases that are not centered primarily on ethical questions.

Simulations

Both simple simulations such as Rubin's role-plays and more extensive, sometimes Web-based simulations of complex business ideas and practices are widespread in business education and distinctive of the field. We saw many kinds of simulations used in the business classes we visited and, notably, none in the arts and sciences classes. It might seem that simulations are designed to teach practical skills and arts and sciences courses focus on conceptual learning. But, in fact, we observed a number of business simulations focused on abstract concepts.

Inevitably, abstract representations of complex processes and phenomena are somewhat removed from the realities they represent. The instructor's goals, therefore, include helping students grasp the relationship between the simplifying concept and a messier, more complex and idiosyncratic reality. In well-designed simulations, acting out the process that the concept represents conveys the abstraction so vividly and concretely that it becomes both memorable and usable.

Enacting a Concept

Babson's Foundations of Management and Entrepreneurship course, for example, uses a computer-based simulation to help students understand the supply-chain phenomenon known as "the bullwhip effect." This phenomenon refers to the fact that because of delays at each stage of the process it is difficult to synchronize the flow of products in a supply chain and the resulting asynchronies are magnified at each step in the chain, starting with the consumer and working backward, just as the tip of a whip oscillates farther and faster than the handle. Students in this class used the simulation to practice balancing a supply chain under a number of different conditions, competing to see who would be first to achieve a balance. They were completely engaged in the task, concentrating very intently, but also laughing at how difficult it was to achieve a balance. In the process, the students saw firsthand how the bullwhip works. As they increased production, they had too much of the product so they had to lower production, causing the system to oscillate.

This kind of dramatic enactment makes abstractions come alive, which is a good thing, but it is a tricky one as well. Concepts can sometimes become so real that students confuse conceptual tools with the reality they represent. The need, then, is for a balanced approach: activities that make theoretical concepts real in combination with activities in which students learn, through Multiple Framing, that concepts are human creations—intellectual tools that are theoretically, historically, culturally, and ideologically contingent.

The bullwhip effect is, of course, a phenomenon within the larger field of business operations and it represents well the emphasis modern business places on efficiency and the use of distributed supply chains to achieve that goal. If somewhere in the curriculum a sophisticated grasp of how efficient supply chains work is combined with consideration of their history, global implications, and other unexamined assumptions, learning will be concrete and usable but also expansive and flexible. We saw some business courses that convey this kind of contextual understanding of concepts, but in most programs they are not prevalent enough to strongly shape student experience.

Simulations and the Development of Social Intelligence

Simulations can also help bring alive for students the social and emotional dynamics of questions that are more typically discussed from a disengaged, decontextualized perspective. As students simulate actual business practices while working together on cases or other projects, they begin to develop skills that are important for business but also the perspective, identity, and even some of the emotional tone of business persons.

When used effectively, this kind of experience can help students better appreciate the importance of trust, integrity, and consideration of others in their business dealings. It can also be helpful for students to gain a heightened appreciation of the fast-paced, complicated, dynamic, and competitive nature of business so they have a realistic sense of the demands their future work environments are likely to make on them. It is important to keep these two sides of the equation in balance or at least in communication with each other. Otherwise, highly competitive simulations such as the Mike's Bikes game used in Introduction to Business at Santa Clara (described in Chapter Three) may socialize students into a rather cut-throat, "take no prisoners" approach to their future work.

The social and emotional authenticity of simulations makes them effective tools for preparing students to act ethically, even when under pressure to cut corners. Simulations that involve role-playing can place students inside complex ethical conflicts, calling up a wider and more authentic range of motives, perceptions, and reactions than an analytical discussion of ethical dilemmas can do. Joel Rubin's use of informal role-playing at the end of the case discussions in the business ethics class we described previously shows how such activities can add emotional depth to complex ethical problems.

Professor Jeanne Enders at Portland State University uses a more formal online role-playing simulation in her Business Environments class to help students understand the different interests, experiences, and concerns of employees in a company. In this simulation, each student is assigned a role, and together they must come to a group consensus for an outside "social auditor" played by the instructor. They do this by interacting with each other online during a two-week period.

When Enders assigns the roles, she tells the students what their character's motivations will be and their grades depend in part on how well they represent those motivations in the role-play. Some employees feel cheated by the company, for example, and others have a vested interest in the company being very profitable. Students are assessed based on the extent of their participation; the quality, timeliness, and relevance of their posts; the application of course concepts; and their fidelity to assigned roles.

Enders believes that engaging ethical questions through this kind of simulation makes a different kind of contribution to student learning than classroom discussions alone can do. She finds that in class discussions of ethical issues students have a tendency to come to obvious and easy "right answers." Because students in these discussions are not subject to the pressures of real business situations, their easy answers may not translate into action under more challenging circumstances. In addition, when the delineations of ethical and unethical behavior are especially subtle and ambiguous, as they are in the simulation, students come to a deeper appreciation of human frailty and complexity than classroom discussions of moral dilemmas usually provide. Enders also takes ethical decision making to the next level of personal relevance by asking students to send her a 250-word "Friday Letter" each week, describing how they have applied a course concept to their own lives. Through this and other mechanisms, the course employs the Reflective Exploration of Meaning as well as Analytical Thinking and Multiple Framing.

Teaching Written and Oral Communication

Teamwork, supervised practice, case studies, and simulations are not mutually exclusive; they often intersect in ways that lead to even more powerful and more integrated liberal learning and business outcomes. In our campus visits, we were struck by an additional element that runs through these pedagogies of enactment: attention to written and oral communication. Often, in fact, these skills are taught in ways that offer particularly useful examples of the cycle of practice and feedback we describe throughout this chapter.

Business Writing

Although some business courses use simulations to support the full range of liberal learning outcomes, as Enders does at Portland State University, it is far from commonplace. More often, simulations are used to teach concrete skills of practice and one of the most prevalent among these is business writing. Courses in business communications often include assignments in which students play various roles, writing cover letters as if applying for a job, drafting business correspondence from within a company, composing various kinds of internal memos and reports, or developing business plans that seek funding for new ventures.

In MIT Sloan School's Managerial Communication course, students write a cover letter for a real job that interests them as well as a number of letters and memos that connect with hypothetical scenarios. For example, they write two memos in which they help implement a policy shift recently mandated within their department. This requires writing one memo to introduce a new calendar-management software package to their somewhat technology-averse boss and another to explain the software to their coworkers and persuade them to accept a mandatory shift to the new system. Later, students in this course work in teams to write longer documents, preparing a grant proposal or a marketing analysis.

In this kind of business communications course, students practice exactly the kind of writing skills they are likely to need on the job. When the courses are well done, as MIT's is, performance criteria are explicit from the outset and students are given feedback on their writing in relation to those criteria. Students, therefore, learn to write in ways that are carefully aligned with the document's purpose, audience, special circumstances, and the like. Students gain a great deal of practical expertise in these courses, an outcome that is clearly important to prospective employers, who often lament that recent college graduates have not learned to write.

These kinds of writing assignments are valuable partly because they are so precisely targeted, helping students learn the sometimes subtle conventions of writing for different purposes in different circumstances. But simulation-type writing assignments can also be structured to expand rather than focus students' perspectives. Like most accounting courses, Advanced Financial Accounting at Indiana University emphasizes the preparation and interpretation of financial statements that pertain to business combinations and partnerships, derivatives, and related issues. The semester ends with a group project in which students consider the stock price and performance data for an actual business combination. This orientation to technical skills is typical of the business curriculum.

Somewhat less typical is the final project's goal of "inspiring students to look beyond a sterile accounting-centered world and to appreciate the substance of the events for which they are accounting." In order to achieve this, the project requires students to work together to write a report evaluating the companies involved in a business combination, the stock market reaction to the combination, the performance of the newly combined entity, and its overall success. Thus, the writing assignment requires students to place their knowledge of financial accounting into a broader business context in order to appreciate the significance of the financial statements they are learning to prepare.

As important as these kinds of experiences are for students, even the wider lens of the final paper for Advanced Financial Accounting raises issues about what the business writing curriculum leaves out as well as what it accomplishes. In terms of our three essential liberal learning outcomes, it seems that the kind of writing that predominates for undergraduate business majors is strong in fostering Analytical Thinking. It is less clear that these writing assignments are well aligned with the other two liberal learning modes of thought we have stressed, Multiple Framing and the Reflective Exploration of Meaning. It is therefore worth considering what kind of writing could address those outcomes and asking whether the inclusion of a wider range of assignments might provide a more complete college education for business majors.

Writing as Inquiry

Teaching writing as a set of practical communication skills is relatively common and often well done in the business curriculum. But there is another important kind of writing that is more likely to be addressed in liberal arts and sciences courses, especially in the humanities, and seems virtually absent in standard business courses. Purdue University professors Janice Lauer and J. William Asher identify this important kind of writing as *rhetorical inquiry* (1988). This approach assumes that written discourse can not only communicate knowledge but also create it.

Writing as inquiry is most likely to be represented in undergraduate research papers or extended essays, but these assignments don't always treat writing as inquiry. Lauer points out that many research papers or essay assignments urge students to start with a thesis. The problem is that this approach neglects entirely the source of the thesis and its relationship to inquiry, issues that are critical in serious scholarship. By contrast, writing as inquiry begins with the formulation of a genuine question that arises from investigation of a substantive concern and that if addressed effectively can help advance the field's understanding of that concern.

The task of writing as inquiry, therefore, begins with the careful identification of a productive question, proceeds through research and investigation to construct a satisfying answer, formulates claims based on these explorations, and constructs arguments to elaborate and support these claims, insights, and judgments. This is a lengthy and demanding process. Even formulating productive questions involves expertise that students must learn through an iterative sequence of practice, feedback, and response. For this reason, this kind of writing assignment is employed infrequently even in the arts and sciences.

The rewards for this kind of work, done well, are great. Writing as inquiry is almost uniquely valuable for combining a disciplined yet creative orientation with the consideration of multiple points of view; hidden cultural and other assumptions; forces that have shaped one's own and others' views, values, and attitudes; and the exploration of meaning in relation to consequential and challenging questions. If we consider what the expertise being demonstrated is, what students are being asked to practice, and on what dimensions they are given guidance and feedback, the contrast between writing for inquiry and practical genres of business writing is dramatic. In our view, both are important components of a full undergraduate education.

It is probably significant that more than anywhere else except some humanities courses we saw writing as inquiry in hybrid courses, those that bring a liberal learning perspective to questions that are significant to the world of business. One such course is The Good Steward, a seminar offered by the Liberal Arts and Management Program at Indiana University. The course explores the phenomenon of stewardship—the careful management of resources for others' benefit—by drawing on sources as varied as the Bible, the literature of the environmental sustainability movement, writings about nonprofit management and fidelity in personal and family affairs, essays by prominent thinkers and historical figures, interviews with political leaders, and Supreme Court decisions.

Among other things, students in this course write a 3,500-word research paper. The writing process involves multiple stages and drafts, each of which is the subject of feedback and revision. The course syllabus notes that "choosing a topic is only the beginning. Isolating a question is the next step in writing a paper and perhaps the hardest." After working with the instructor to identify a question, students must submit an abstract that explains the significance of the question and suggests a strategy for investigating and constructing a credible answer. Overall, the process takes two months. This is a far cry from the short, relatively simple assignments employed in most business writing courses. Although it is not realistic to expect that all or even most college courses will engage students in this kind of sustained inquiry, we believe it is both realistic and imperative that all college students carry out this kind of work frequently enough to gain at least a beginning expertise in the kind of deep, creative inquiry it represents.

Two Views of Oral Communication

In a close parallel with the contrasting approaches to writing we have just described, the teaching of oral communication takes pragmatic and investigative forms in undergraduate education. In a telling conversation at MIT, a humanities faculty member on the curriculum review committee commented that faculty from both professional and arts and sciences disciplines agree on the importance of oral communication skills but that the two groups may have quite different conceptions of what these skills include. According to the observer, faculty from engineering and the Sloan School of Management are more likely to associate communication with skills of presentation: communicating to an audience the procedures and results of formal problem solving. In contrast, faculty from the humanities, arts, and social sciences departments tend to think of oral communication skills as primarily the ability to learn and persuade by discussion: to become skilled in using discussion as a medium of deliberation and dialectical discovery. In this, they are evoking an iconic conception of liberal education. In the view of Robert Maynard Hutchins, the philosopher of education and legendary president of the University of Chicago in the 1930s and 1940s, seminars—settings dedicated to deliberation and exchange—are the sine qua non of liberal education. He argued that seminars built around seminal works of western civilization were the basis for what he termed *the great conversation* (Hutchins, 1955).

This perspective on liberal learning is still current in contemporary higher education. The idea is that coming to understand ideas, careful argumentation, different ways of framing an issue, and social or personal meaning is not exclusively an individual or solitary activity; conversation with others is an essential pedagogy of liberal learning. The greater prevalence of seminars that engage students deeply with collaborative investigation of ideas may, thus, account for the fact that humanities and social science majors are much more likely to report that they have learned from perspectives different from their own than do students in business and engineering—despite their focus on teamwork (National Survey of Student Engagement, 2010). The explanation may be that the task orientation of most teamwork entails less real engagement with unfamiliar perspectives than does the kind of extended conversation that takes place in seminars.

This kind of conversation is not achieved by instructors interrupting their lectures periodically to ask whether there are any comments or questions. Instead, it requires the authentic exchange of ideas among students, attentive and insightful listening to each other, and a sustained practice of responding to and building on others' arguments. Productive discussions of this sort do not happen without skilled guidance from the instructor. Like any demanding pedagogy, including other high-quality pedagogies of enactment, seminar discussions require explicit attention to process and desired outcomes.

Engagement with Narrative Texts

Seminar-type discussions in which participants share different perspectives help students trace through the logic of alternative representations, trying on different theoretical, historical, and cultural lenses. Seminars are often organized around texts of various kinds, including the full range of literary modes. As we discussed in Chapter Four, a particularly significant mode for liberal learning is that of narrative—texts that tell stories. Narrative texts of various kinds serve as the stimulus not only for seminar discussions but also for writing and other kinds of student activity.

In thinking about a story's meaning, the reader pulls out certain features from the narrative, treating them as instances of more general categories, which then make possible various comparisons and contrasts across categories. As they work through these applications of Analytical Thinking to narrative material, students learn to use formal thinking to make sense of both routine and unusual life events. When students present their analyses to the instructor and their classmates, they come to see that the same narrative can be understood from multiple perspectives and often supports several alternative interpretations.

At the same time, students are often emotionally engaged with the issues presented in the narrative, identifying with one or more characters and their predicaments. As students imagine themselves on different life paths, with different values and sensibilities, they can explore the meaning of these alternatives for their own aspirations and commitments. Therefore, as we discuss in Chapter Four, engagement with narrative is an important contributor to our third mode of liberal learning, the Reflective Exploration of Meaning.

To this end, the Professional Responsibility and Leadership course that caps the NYU Stern School's Social Impact Core uses literary works by Anton Chekhov, Walt Whitman, and others to engage students with questions of identity, values, and life purpose. Early in the course, students read Chekhov's story "Gooseberries," which tells the tale of a man who sacrifices everything to get something he really wants: a farm that raises gooseberries. The narrator in the story is the farmer's brother and, from his point of view, the farmer has wasted his life. The story raises questions about the meaning of happiness; the values of social contribution, comfort, and beauty; and the relationship of these values to personal happiness. In doing so, the story provides a context for students to ask themselves how they define a meaningful life, what they are willing to sacrifice for, and what is worth doing. Some students may identify with the narrator, others with his brother. In either case, they must explicate the character's perspective and imagine themselves facing comparable life choices as well as thinking through the significance of the text on a more general or abstract level.

Although works of fiction are the most familiar narrative texts, history, philosophy, and the more reflective, interpretive forms of writing from the social and natural sciences (think of Stephen J. Gould, Oliver Sacks, and others) can also take the form of narratives, as can films and other media that draw on narrative forms. In all of these domains, historical figures, groups, institutions, and even abstract forces can serve as characters in the story. Regardless of the nature of the story and its characters, the pedagogy and its purposes remain analogous: to generate insight through taking multiple points of view and to assist students in moving toward various forms of accommodation of those differing perspectives. At its best, the inclusive, integrated perspective that results represents a more universal sympathy and understanding.

In order to make unfamiliar perspectives come alive for students, vivid narrative modes such as fiction or films can be particularly effective. In The Philosophy of Work, Bentley University philosophy professor Carolyn Magid immerses students in narrative modes on and off throughout the semester. In addition to using fiction and other narrative texts, Magid shows the film *Clockwork* to help students learn about the emergence and influence of Frederick Taylor's scientific management approach in the early twentieth century. Before seeing this film, most students were unaware of Taylor's influential and controversial role in the history of management. Watching and discussing the film makes Taylor's approach real for students who otherwise lack a historical perspective on contemporary approaches to management.

Also in Magid's course, students read Bebe Moore Campbell's novel, *Brothers and Sisters*, which tells the story of men and women of different races connected with a bank in Los Angeles (Campbell, 1995). The story is set shortly after the 1992 riots in Los Angeles following the acquittal of police officers who had been filmed beating an African American man named Rodney King. Through the book's fictional account of a superficial diversity awareness program implemented by the bank, students come to appreciate the very different points of view that individuals from different cultural backgrounds bring to a shared experience and work toward their own judgments about the difficult and contested issues raised by this novel.

An Integrated Approach to Communication Skills

If undergraduate business students do not engage in writing for inquiry and in seminar-type discussions as well as more skills-based business communications courses, it is hard to say that they have had a full liberal education. These pedagogies should be experienced in the liberal arts and sciences courses that business students take but we believe they also belong in the business curriculum. If they are segregated on the liberal education side—into what some students call *opinion courses*—they are likely to be written off as irrelevant to the "real business of business." Yet inquiry, creativity, and an expanded worldview are important elements of the most effective approaches to commerce as well as other domains of human life. The capacity to connect these deeper modes of inquiry with topics of obvious relevance to business is a special contribution of programs such as Indiana University's Liberal Arts and Management Program; Franklin & Marshall's Business, Organizations, and Society program; and other efforts to connect liberal learning directly and intentionally with the preparation for business.

O

In these kinds of pedagogies—writing as rhetorical inquiry, seminars, and engagement with narrative texts—business faculty can learn a lot from their arts and sciences colleagues about how to connect Analytical Thinking with narrative material, help students learn to deal with ambiguity, and teach for Multiple Framing and the Reflective Exploration of Meaning in a grounded and disciplined manner. Similarly, arts and sciences faculty can learn a great deal from business faculty about how to make sure that students' academic learning is really usable for engaging with complex, real-world problems. For that, students need to develop Practical Reasoning, judgment, and a whole range of skills, including those of working productively with others in teams. The pedagogies of enactment that are so prevalent in undergraduate business education and so often skillfully executed ought to provide models for arts and sciences faculty who wish to consider more carefully what forms of expertise they are trying to teach and how to help students practice that expertise in a directed, guided, self-conscious way.

If this happens, we believe that learning in the arts and sciences disciplines will be greatly enriched, becoming more exciting and engaging for arts and sciences majors as well as for professional and vocational majors who take courses in these disciplines. By combining the immediacy of learning to draw on academic knowledge for practice with the intellectual excitement of exploration and discovery, professional and vocational majors and those in the arts and sciences can all gain a fuller, more socially and individually promising preparation for life.

We are convinced that the best efforts to connect liberal and business learning are both models and vehicles for bringing faculty together in pursuit of this educational vision. With this possibility in view, we turn in Chapter Seven to designs that ensure such connections not simply at the level of the individual course or assignment but also through curricular design and other cross-cutting structural features of education.

7

STRUCTURAL APPROACHES TO INTEGRATION

BUILDING INSTITUTIONAL INTENTIONALITY

IT SHOULD BE CLEAR from previous chapters that undergraduate business programs can offer rich opportunities for students to engage with high-quality liberal learning—in business courses themselves, in the arts and sciences, and in hybrid experiences that combine the two. Not surprisingly, given our theme of integration, we believe that the strongest preparation includes work in all three of these. It must also include mechanisms to help students connect their learning across the various areas of the undergraduate experience.

Developing an educational program that integrates liberal and business learning requires careful thought, resources, and, perhaps most important, institutional intentionality. The default approach—a set of distribution requirements within which students choose courses in several arts and sciences disciplines—does not ensure a well-integrated whole. Given the drive to gain career-related skills and knowledge, these requirements are unlikely to be a high priority for students—or even for faculty. In fact, one dean we spoke with suggested that students should choose at least one course in the arts and sciences with nothing more to recommend it than its minimal workload.

Throughout our visits to business schools, we saw the critical importance of institutionally intentional steps to promote the integration of business and liberal learning. With such intentionality, we believe that any campus can strengthen the liberal education of its business students. Without it, some business students will find their way through a strong liberal education but this will be largely a matter of chance, with low odds and high stakes. What is also clear is that without institutional intentionality, opportunities for exploration and growth are crowded out by the pressure students feel to pursue as many business-related credentials as they can manage.

Fortunately, some undergraduate business programs have designed and implemented creative strategies to make sure their students engage with the essential dimensions of liberal learning and bring its intellectual richness to their preparation as business professionals, individuals, and citizens. There are many different ways to do this and the most powerful approaches are those that emerge from the institution's unique mission, history, resources, and circumstances.

Across the variety of possible approaches, however, curriculum is always an essential element. That is, student learning can benefit from the pedagogical choices made by *individual* instructors—as illustrated by the courses and experiences featured in the previous several chapters. But a truly integrated experience requires more than individual choices; it requires *structural* attention within a *program* of courses and experiences that build on one another and add up to a powerfully integrated student experience. In this sense, carefully structured curricula are the single most powerful route for ensuring that business students engage with and learn to use the rich substantive content of the arts and sciences along with the modes of thinking we have called Analytical Thinking, Multiple Framing, and the Reflective Exploration of Meaning, all culminating in the capacity for wise Practical Reasoning.

In this chapter, then, we will describe two main categories of curricular structure designed to ensure liberal learning and to integrate it with preparation for business. These structures are often accompanied by other processes that can support their aims and we will describe two of these: targeted systems of student advising and programs for faculty development. Additionally, we will examine cocurricular aspects of student life and the institutional culture as significant variables that support (or sometimes undermine) curricular efforts toward integration.

Curricular Models and Approaches

The two major curricular models we encountered in our study reflect a fundamental institutional choice: whether to prepare students for business within the structure of the arts and sciences or to offer a designated business school or program separate from arts and sciences departments. Clearly, this choice depends on many factors, and it is not unusual for an institution to move from one of these approaches to the other (in either direction) or even to have both kinds of programs. Indiana University, for example, has a business school that offers undergraduate degrees and a business-preparation program within the arts and sciences.

Our intent here is not to compare the advantages and disadvantages of these two models; what works best is largely a function of institutional fit. Our aim is rather to illustrate how both kinds of programs can succeed in integrating liberal and business learning if they bring sufficient commitment and intentionality to the task. We will consider programs in business schools first and then turn to programs that are located within arts and sciences faculties or schools.

Approaches That Expand and Enrich Business Education Programs

Business majors are typically enrolled in a business school or program for two or more of their undergraduate years. In many cases, their experience is a sort of mini-MBA program with the distinctive features of an undergraduate education submerged along the way. But some institutions are acutely aware of what is lost in this kind of approach. They offer strong preparation for business and they also commit to an enriched and expanded version of that preparation, one that takes liberal learning seriously as the basis for thoughtful approaches to business and to life beyond the office. In our site visits, we identified a number of dynamic examples, looking especially at those that find ways to reach all or most of their students.

PROGRAMMATIC EMPHASIS ON SOCIAL IMPACT. One way to expand and enrich business education is to widen business students' angle of vision by paying explicit and sustained attention to the effects of business on society and, conversely, the effects of society on business. The Stern School of Business at New York University, with strong support from the dean and senior faculty, has adopted a required four-course curricular sequence that addresses these themes in different ways during each of the students' four undergraduate years. The courses focus explicitly on the formation of students' professional responsibility, character, and thoughtfulness about the place of business in the larger social context. Thus, in their freshman year, all Stern students take Business and Its Publics, followed, in the sophomore year, by Organizational Communication and Its Social Context. As juniors, they study Law, Business, and Society, and in their senior year they take a capstone course entitled Professional Responsibility and Leadership. It is worth looking at these one by one to appreciate the way they build on and reinforce one another.

The freshman year course combines a plenary lecture series with small-group discussions and writing classes to introduce students to the interconnections among business, society, markets, politics, religion, art, and life. This kind of introduction to business is a far cry from the more typical freshman course, which provides overviews of the major business disciplines but rarely steps back to consider the wider meaning and contexts of business as one social institution among many. As sophomores, students study social processes of influence and persuasion and learn how to communicate effectively with a wide range of stakeholders. In their junior year, they learn about the role of law in shaping and governing the conduct of business and the global impact of commerce.

The series culminates in the capstone course, Professional Responsibility and Leadership, which we have described in some detail in previous chapters. This course asks students to think about their careers in relation to their broader sense of self, their values, and purposes in life. In the view of faculty director, Bruce Buchanan, the capstone is an essential experience as the students prepare to embark on their life's work: "It's amazing to me how early they shut out a lot of options. I want them to see that they have choices."

By making social impact a required part of its core curriculum for the entire four years, the Stern School is enacting its institutional judgment that these issues are of critical importance to a well-educated business professional. The program requires a major commitment of resources and benefits from the enthusiastic leadership of Sally Blount, the dean at the time of our visit, and a number of distinguished senior faculty. In order to reach the entire student body, some sections are taught by adjunct faculty but the leaders of the four courses are senior faculty and adjuncts are carefully chosen and well prepared.

We believe that this program, though distinctive to Stern, could be adapted for use in other business programs if it were tailored to fit their specific goals and resources. Much of its power at NYU derives from the fact that all students participate but in some settings it might be more feasible or appropriate to offer this kind of experience as an elective. In fact, the Wharton School at the University of Pennsylvania offers an elective program with some of the same aims; Social Impact and Responsibility is a secondary concentration, which means that students can choose it but that it cannot be their primary focus. As at Stern, the Wharton program entails four courses: (1) a foundation course, Social

Impact and Responsibility, which provides an overview of issues and intellectual tools for examining business from a socially oriented perspective; (2) a focus course (students can chose among several possibilities including Urban Fiscal Policy, Comparative Healthcare Systems, and Corporate Responsibility and Ethics), which teaches the frameworks and background knowledge needed to understand a specific approach to generating social value; (3) an application course designed to build concrete skills that students can apply in generating social value, such as Entrepreneurship and Societal Wealth Venturing; and (4) an elective chosen from a number of relevant categories. Except for the foundation course, the elements of this program already existed in the Wharton curriculum, a circumstance that clearly facilitates its implementation.

LINKING ARTS AND SCIENCES WITH BUSINESS COURSES. A different curricular approach requires students to take courses that explicitly link business and other fields in order to explore more deeply a set of issues of particular interest to the student. This approach has been adopted by Santa Clara University, where a new core curriculum was introduced in fall 2009. Integration is a major theme of the core, and the principal vehicle for integration is called *Pathways* in which students choose three or four courses with a common, interdisciplinary theme. These courses and associated experiences are meant to help students reflect on the learning process itself and on their vocational and educational choices from the perspectives of several disciplines. Pathways clusters include Vocation; Sustainability; Democracy; Leading People, Organizations, and Social Change; Public Policy; and Food, Hunger, Poverty, and the Environment. The courses that make up these clusters are created specifically for the Pathways program.

This means that business students, like students in other majors, explicitly connect the learning in their majors with what they are learning in a wide range of other disciplines, especially the liberal arts and sciences. Many Santa Clara faculty refer to the structure of this curriculum as a double helix (an image we borrow throughout this book) because it thoroughly and consistently integrates vocational and other majors with the broader curriculum. The aim is for students to see the liberal arts and sciences dimensions of professional fields (business and others) and understand how liberal learning can enrich and deepen engagement with the world. The power of the experience for students is best illustrated by concrete examples.

Barry Posner, former dean of Santa Clara's Leavey School of Business and author of influential works on leadership, leads a Pathways sequence called Leading People, Organizations, and Social Change. The sequence, which is open to students in the arts and sciences as well as business, is designed to examine theories of leadership and to cultivate the skills and competencies needed to lead people and organizations to achieve social change. Students in the program are exposed to historical and contemporary leaders and their impact, exploring the methods leaders use to inspire and accomplish change in various roles and settings. Throughout the experience, students are challenged to reflect on the type of leader they believe they should become in order to achieve their own goals while also addressing the needs of the greater community.

Another Pathways sequence called Democracy is noteworthy for broadening a set of issues that is especially likely to go unexamined in business education, to the serious detriment of students' development. The prospectus for this cluster suggests that "a business major might argue for his or her vision of whether shareholders, employees, customers, or citizens should have stronger or weaker rights to influence corporations' decisions or examine how economic theories of democracy (such as those of Anthony Downs or Joseph Schumpeter) could be applied to contemporary issues" (Santa Clara University, 2009).

Of course, it is not necessary to rework the entire general education program in order to develop sets of linked courses that provide students with thoughtful perspectives on business and society. Bentley University, for example, draws on already existing courses to create a thematically based curricular option called the Liberal Studies Major (LSM). This program follows a deceptively simple design, one that could, we believe, be adopted fairly easily by other colleges and universities. Bentley students choose from among interdisciplinary themes such as American Perspectives, Ethics and Social Responsibility, Global Perspectives, Health and Industry, Media Arts and Society, and Workplace and Labor Studies. Because virtually all Bentley students major in business, each theme addresses connections of the thematic topic with business.

Each participating student also has an LSM advisor with expertise in the student's chosen concentration. Students work with the advisor to select a set of eight courses that represents their theme. At least six of the eight must be from arts and sciences departments, with no more than four from any one discipline. In addition to taking these courses, each year students write an analytical essay that is directed and assessed by the advisor and included in an electronic portfolio representing the student's work in LSM. At the end of the program, students complete a culminating experience designed to unify their studies in the concentration, again under the direction of their faculty advisor.

One important consequence of the LSM curricular design, similar to the general education approach at Santa Clara, is that students bring their insights from different courses together in a dialogue, internally and with others. In the absence of a structure to support that integration, students may learn in separate courses about the ways that various disciplines or subdisciplines frame their major questions, methods, and interpretations but they may not even notice that different frames offer conflicting perspectives, let alone learn to resolve those conflicting points of view through a synthetic integration. Bentley's Liberal Studies Major and other integrative programs featured here are valuable precisely because they provide institutionally structured arrangements to facilitate intentional connections and integrations.

Not coincidentally, there has been an explosion of student interest in LSM since it was instituted at Bentley a few years ago. Five hundred students signed up for the program by the end of the second year. What explains this interest? Students we talked to see LSM as a relatively easy way to gain added coherence in their Bentley education and to get a liberal education credential in the process. Some of these students, who have, after all, chosen to attend a business-focused college, worry about what they have given up by pursuing a business rather than liberal arts degree. The LSM program helps them fill in some of what they think they would otherwise miss. Many students also feel that what they learn through the particular topic of their LSM concentration, such as globalization or health care, informs and shapes their preparation for business in important ways, even pointing to career tracks they discovered through the program. An accounting student who took the Ethics and Social Responsibility LSM told us, for instance, how excited he had become about forensic accounting, a field he had not heard of before he started the program but now plans to pursue.

Approaches to Business Preparation Within the Arts and Sciences

Many college students in all kinds of institutions want to prepare for careers in business. The most obvious way to do this is to major in business in a college or university with a business school or department. But this is not the only way. Some institutions provide business-preparation programs that are located within the arts and sciences. This model shifts the focus, making the arts and sciences central and embedding the study of business within that frame. Business as an institution—how it is organized, how it operates, and how it affects and is affected by other social institutions—becomes the arena for study. This curricular structure entails a blend of arts and sciences and business disciplines.

BUSINESS, ORGANIZATIONS, AND SOCIETY. Franklin & Marshall College provides an interesting example of how this model can work. This small liberal arts college had previously offered a business degree through a fairly conventional business department. Several years ago, the school, which had many business majors, decided to move the preparation for business into the liberal arts, restructuring and renaming the business department and giving the program's content a clearer liberal learning cast. The new department, Business, Organizations, and Society (BOS), emphasizes that business represents one cluster of organizations among many others in society and helps students explore the mutual influences and interactions between business organizations and other social institutions. The program is impressively intentional in its efforts to infuse arts and sciences disciplines into the study of business, providing perspectives from history, psychology, anthropology, and other social sciences as well as law and the business fields of management, accounting, marketing, and finance.

All BOS majors take an initial course called Organizing in the Twenty-First Century. The course syllabus begins with a telling statement: "Commerce, and indeed most human activity, takes place through a complex network of private, business, public sector, and not-for-profit organizations. The quality of our lives is increasingly contingent upon how effectively we design, plan for, and execute innovative systems, policies, and procedures to facilitate problem solving and decision making" in these diverse institutions. The course aims to teach students about organizational effectiveness through strategic analysis, choice, and implementation. This kind of multidisciplinary introduction to organizations and organizational effectiveness contrasts with standard introductory business courses, which provide brief overviews of accounting, finance, management, and marketing. The faculty member who designed the course explains it with a metaphor: conventional introductions to business lead students to feel as if they need to fit together the pieces of a jigsaw puzzle without having seen a picture of the completed puzzle; the BOS course shows students that picture.

The BOS structure also helps resolve a tension that liberal arts campuses face. On the one hand, many of their students want to be equipped for an occupation on graduation and business is first on the list for most of them. On the other hand, these colleges are deeply rooted in the liberal arts and sciences and their faculties believe passionately in the value of a liberal education. The Franklin & Marshall approach—an arts and sciences–infused preparation for business—enables the college to "have it both ways," in the words of one student who talked with us. Many institutions, including large universities as well as liberal arts colleges, have begun to institute some version of this model.

OPPORTUNITIES FOR EXPLORATION. One example is Indiana University's Liberal Arts and Management Program (LAMP). LAMP starts each year with a new cohort of one hundred honors students in the arts and sciences and provides them with a strong business education: six business courses, which include accounting, marketing, management, and economics. In their freshman, junior, and senior years, LAMP students also take interdisciplinary seminars that connect business with its historical and societal settings. Historian James Madison leads the program and he recruits outstanding faculty from the College of Arts and Sciences and IU's business school as well as from other parts of the university, inviting them to teach a new interdisciplinary course in their field of interest. In Madison's words, LAMP focuses on "the why questions—the larger picture of business and its intersections with society and history." Students, he said, should "be comfortable with gray," moving beyond the inclination to look for clear, black-and-white answers.

LAMP students, though serious about preparing for business careers, also display the kind of exploratory curiosity that is more typical of arts and sciences students, and they value this intellectually curious approach to life. One of these students told us a story that was meant to illustrate this quality in LAMP students. Over the summer he had had a conversation with some friends in IU's business school—highly intelligent people, in his view, who, "three years down the line will be working for Goldman Sachs and McKinsey." The conversation was about dandelions; someone had asked why some dandelions are white on top and some are yellow. The business school students believed that when yellow dandelions die, they become the kind "with the little white things you can blow off." The LAMP student disagreed and turned to a biology major for support in his view that dandelions with white tops are not dead but, instead, going through a natural cycle of reproduction. In response to this explanation, the business students looked at him with blank stares, saying, in effect, "Whatever! That's useless information." They felt that "it doesn't even matter." But, the LAMP student stressed to us, in the best traditions of liberal learning, "It *does* matter. It's very significant, I think, just knowing what's going on in our world." Another LAMP student chimed in, "You should be curious about it." The original student added, "It really bothered me, disturbed me, that these people, . . . some of the most intelligent people I know, were not curious at all. They just brushed me off; it didn't even matter to them."

Programs such as LAMP are not full-scale substitutes for a business major. And LAMP's quality depends in part on attracting high-achieving honors students who bring an abundance of curiosity to their studies. But the program offers a significant way for arts and science students to gain exposure to the core of standard business education while also learning about business in a broader, multidisciplinary context.

Another curricular option for business preparation for arts and sciences students is to offer a minor in business. Northwestern University offers a curricular option that addresses some of the same issues as LAMP, Franklin & Marshall's BOS, and NYU's Social Impact Core, treating business as one kind of social institution that must be understood in a wider historical, social, cultural, and policy context. The Northwestern offering—the Harvey Kapnick Business Institutions Program, as it's called—is part of the College of Arts and Sciences, not the Kellogg School of Business. It has been a hit with students. The program doubled in its first four years and is currently the largest minor at Northwestern, enrolling 8 percent of undergraduates. The university Web site describes the program as "based on the assumption that the study of business can be approached through a thoughtful investigation of the cultural, political, philosophical, literary, and social sources and consequences of business institutions." In contrast to preprofessional training of the usual sort, its intent is to provide a broad, multidisciplinary perspective on the domain of business "as a significant area of inquiry." As such, the program is intentional in linking liberal learning with business education.

To be clear, the Business Institutions minor at Northwestern differs significantly from business minors at most universities that offer them. Typically, the business minor is sponsored by the business school and features a curriculum that is essentially a subset of the courses business majors take. For example, the minor provided by the business school at Arizona State University in Tempe calls for thirty-six credits of specified business courses: twenty-four credits in lower-division courses such as accounting, macroeconomics, and math, and twelve credits in upper-division courses in areas such as finance, management and leadership, and global supply operations. Essentially a compressed business major, this kind of program aims at students who want as much real business education as possible while also majoring in another field.

Some business schools offer minors in particular dimensions of business. At Clemson University, for example, the Spiro Institute offers a minor in entrepreneurship for nonbusiness majors. Along with three core business courses, students may choose one of three tracks—Experiential, Planning, or Foundations—each of which requires two additional courses.

Supporting an Integrative Curriculum

Creating an integrative curriculum that not only supports business and liberal learning but also draws them together in creative ways is a major step forward. But making that curriculum work the way it should requires student buy-in and faculty expertise and commitment. Two key mechanisms for achieving these elements of success—student advising and faculty development—are familiar in higher education, though not always directed toward the goal of integration. Student advising, for example, can strengthen liberal education for business students but it can also undercut it. Absent a commitment to advise students in ways that convey the value of liberal learning, the advising experience is likely to reinforce the narrowly instrumental orientation that characterizes the experience of many business students. Similar to designing curricula, advising must be intentional; the same can be said of faculty development. Strong faculty development programs signal that administrative leaders are serious about teaching for liberal learning and its connections with preparation for work. And, because most faculty are accustomed to teaching practices based in disciplinary conventions, shifting to a new approach requires rethinking, collegial communication, skill development, and reflection. The challenge is to design advising and faculty development in ways that support the integration of liberal learning and business education—and then to implement and sustain them in ways that faithfully reflect that goal.

Student Advising

Many undergraduate business programs, particularly at large universities, employ full-time advisors to counsel students on their academic programs. In an earlier era, advising undergraduates was more likely to be the province of faculty members, but today it is widely believed that professional advisors are in a better position to help students than are faculty, who may be familiar with courses in their own departments but understand little about curricular requirements and opportunities more generally. Certainly professional advisors can be enormously helpful to students trying to put together programs that meet requirements while also matching their particular interests and needs. The problem is that when advisors for business majors are located within the business school, they naturally tend to make the business curriculum a priority. This focus can intensify the degree to which business trumps the liberal arts when students choose courses and other activities and can therefore work against integration.

That said, members of the advising staff, even within business schools, are often themselves liberal arts graduates so they bring to their work an appreciation of the value of intellectual exploration for undergraduates. The challenge is to promote the liberal learning experience in the face of pressure from students to make curricular choices that maximize their attractiveness in a highly competitive job market. Many of the advisors we spoke to underscored what we have called the instrumental orientation of business students. In their experience, these students learn as early as high school that their energy in college should be directed toward whatever will be most appealing to corporate recruiters. Understandably, many advisors feel they must take these concerns seriously and are keenly aware of the challenges students face in meeting their many requirements in general education, the major, and often a second major within the time frame available. The solution, alas, is to advise students to choose their business courses first and fit other offerings in around the edges, often with a view to time slots and workload rather than opportunities for exploration and inquiry.

Clearly advisors are in a difficult bind—one that points to the importance of including them in discussions with administrative leaders and faculty about how to strengthen business students' liberal learning and its connections with business education. Such involvement can help advisors think through how best to convey the excitement and value of liberal learning to students who arrive with a single-minded focus on their short-term prospects in the job market. In turn, advisors' feedback to the curriculum committee and others charged with structuring requirements and schedules can help ensure that creative educational visions can be implemented successfully on the ground.

Joint Faculty Development Programs for Business and Liberal Arts

Most development programs for faculty in a particular discipline are focused on teaching and scholarship in that discipline, and business is no exception. As a result, faculty development programs in business may tend to accentuate any gaps that already exist between the faculties of business and the arts and sciences. Those gaps and their associated tensions may also be magnified by differences in compensation, faculty offices, and other amenities.

At large institutions, faculty members in different schools and departments rarely have occasion to work together except on committees that are unrelated to classroom teaching. Even at small liberal arts colleges, as we heard during our campus visits, there are few incentives for collaboration and there may even be disincentives. In one college, for example, all courses had been taught as three fifty-minute classes per week. Suddenly, without consulting the arts and sciences faculty, the business faculty decided to move to classes that meet twice a week for seventy-five minutes. The purpose of this change was a reasonable one: to achieve longer, more concentrated blocks of time. Its unintended consequence was, however, to make it more difficult for business students to fit arts and sciences courses into their schedules and for arts and sciences students to take business courses. This is just one of many ways that business and arts and sciences departments can diverge if attention is not given to bringing them together.

The good news is that some schools have now put in place programs that promote constructive interaction between liberal arts and business faculties. These efforts are, admittedly, not yet widespread, but they are worth considering because they serve several important functions and are appealing to faculty if well run. One model entails multidisciplinary faculty development seminars—often sponsored by a centralized teaching and learning center—which help participants take a wider view of their teaching and stimulate them to rethink the goals and methods of existing and newly developed courses. When business and liberal arts faculty come together in these settings, the likelihood of weaving together liberal learning and business is greatly enhanced and tensions among faculty from the two domains are reduced.

In recent years, Bentley University—where (like Babson) virtually all students are business majors—has made a major effort to encourage arts and sciences faculty to talk with business faculty about liberal education and to help business faculty weave liberal learning throughout their courses. The catalyst for this effort was a set of week-long faculty workshops funded by a local foundation. The workshops were voluntary and those who participated received a stipend. Each workshop had roughly half business and half arts and sciences faculty, and each day focused on a key issue that cut across business and the liberal arts and sciences:

social responsibility and ethics, communication and information technology, global citizenship, different approaches to critical thinking, and service to the community.

The Davis Workshops (the Davis Foundation funded them) encouraged business faculty to develop new approaches to their teaching in ways that explicitly draw on the arts and sciences while those in the arts and sciences were supported in their efforts to include and integrate business issues. Toward these ends, faculty were asked to comment critically on the syllabi of colleagues from other fields. According to faculty members we talked with, this kind of exchange led to a heightened emphasis on interdisciplinary course design as well as to some joint research projects. Even though the workshops did not continue after the two-year grant period, sufficient numbers of faculty had participated to constitute a critical mass of program alums. Their work, in turn, has been facilitated by the Valente Center, which provides support for interdisciplinary research and innovative teaching, emphasizing links between arts and sciences and business. Each year the Center adopts a broad theme—such as the political economy of the common good—and five faculty are given fellowships that provide a reduced teaching load and help in developing interdisciplinary research projects and teaching proposals that relate to society, the economy, and business.

Yet another route to the integration of liberal learning with business education lies in the institutional acculturation and support of new faculty members. This is what Franklin & Marshall College has done through a development program that prepares new faculty members to teach what are called Foundations courses, two of which must be taken by freshmen. These interdisciplinary courses are designed to show beginning students how "big ideas" tie together different realms of scholarship and to help them develop the values and attributes they will need for life and work. For example, a course called What Work Is traces changing concepts of work over time. Taught by an economist, it draws on history, economics, anthropology, psychology, and other social sciences and humanities to give students multiple perspectives on the overarching question around which the course is organized.

Before teaching a Foundations course, faculty members participate in a grant-funded summer seminar during which they are coached on strategies for teaching this kind of integrative course. In the seminars, faculty share suggestions for readings, exchange ideas about course content and design, and try out possible class activities. Participants' varied backgrounds lead to hard thinking about the assumptions they bring to their courses and the pedagogies they will use, and they receive feedback from their peers and from the lead instructor. Led each year by a faculty member who participated in the prior year, these faculty development seminars are an institutionally intentional effort to build up a common culture of intellectual inquiry. Particularly powerful for new faculty in the Business, Organizations, and Society program (because graduate training for most of them is in business), the seminars reinforce the liberal arts culture of Franklin & Marshall in ways that make a real difference for students.

The Cocurriculum and the Campus Culture

The undergraduate curriculum does not exist in a vacuum. Student learning is also strongly shaped by cocurricular experiences and by the campus culture or climate in which both classroom and out-of-class experiences take place. The cocurriculum and the campus culture can significantly strengthen the liberal learning of undergraduate business students or they can magnify the ways in which business education undervalues students' learning in the liberal arts and sciences fields. These two dimensions are treated separately in the paragraphs that follow but it is important to recognize the many ways that the two can be mutually reinforcing, for better or worse. If the goal is to strengthen liberal learning for all students, including those in vocational or professional majors, it is worth investing in efforts that will create positive synergies among the curriculum, the cocurriculum, and the campus culture.

Cocurricular Activities

For many students, the most important educational experiences in college take place not in the classroom but on the school newspaper, in student government, or in clubs promoting the arts, sports, or social causes such as environmentalism. These cocurricular experiences are especially powerful at residential campuses but even at institutions in which most students commute they can be valuable learning experiences. In fact, in undergraduate education generally, research shows that students' cocurricular involvement is directly linked to the amount of time they spend on campus, the quality of that experience, and their persistence in college (Astin, 1985). And, in this regard, business majors are no different from their peers in other fields. A recent study of undergraduate business majors shows that their satisfaction with their programs at the time of graduation depends more on their satisfaction with cocurricular activities than with their assessments of teaching quality in the subject matter or student advising (Letcher & Neves, 2010).

Precisely because they are so engaging, cocurricular activities for business students can either reinforce the insularity of business education or they can strengthen central elements of liberal learning. Professionally oriented clubs such as those in accounting or marketing are popular among business students, as are business-case competitions. Accounting clubs, for example, help their members learn about the field of accounting as it is actually practiced and provide good contacts with accounting firms for prospective job applicants. Similarly, business-case competitions teach useful skills and can be a way for business students to add another "decoration" to their resumes, as a business-student advisor at one large university noted. These are educationally useful activities. But activities that orient directly toward the job market can heighten the instrumental pressures that business students already feel. Winning a case competition may help on the road to the first job but it is less likely to encourage students to reach beyond business school boundaries and explore. Likewise, spending one's free time in clubs or other activities that attract only business majors can prevent students from experiencing the full richness of the college environment.

To be clear, we are not dismissing the value of these and other cocurricular activities that take place largely within business schools. Our point is that they need to be intentionally designed and guided by faculty with an eye toward supporting students' broader learning and with a commitment to goals that go beyond the instrumental. This possibility was on display at several programs we visited. In fact, students on many campuses participate in socially responsible investment clubs that teach them sound investment practices while taking social impact into account.

An example of this type of program is the Virtu project, started by students in Indiana University's Liberal Arts and Management Program (LAMP) who wanted to put their liberal education to work. Students seek voluntary pledges from IU alumni and pretend to invest the pledged funds in a portfolio of carefully selected instruments. Participating alumni agree to give to a designated local charity an amount equal to 10 percent of what the portfolio would have earned if the investment had been real; the University Foundation handles the finances. As one LAMP student told us, Virtu is "a conduit for learning and a mechanism for change."

Cocurricular activities provide especially powerful learning experiences when they are also explicitly linked to the curriculum. Babson College, for example, connects curricular and cocurricular learning through its Coaching for Leadership and Teamwork Program (CLTP). Student participation in this cocurricular program begins in the first year and is directed toward helping students develop skills and personal qualities that complement what they are learning through their coursework. CLTP provides assessment and coaching on leadership, teamwork, decision making, oral communication, and listening. By taking part in the program at the beginning of their undergraduate years and repeating the experience as juniors, students can set goals, track their progress, and redouble their efforts when they see areas that still need improvement.

Morehouse College also takes leadership and teamwork development very seriously and connects curricular and cocurricular supports for that development. Sophomores at Morehouse take a required management course in which they develop a "leadership portfolio" that must include, among other items, a report on their ongoing participation in a cocurricular club. As a result, we learned, students are encouraged to engage in cocurricular activities and to think about those activities as leadership-learning experiences.

Of course, many cocurricular activities that attract business students are located outside the business school and also involve students majoring in other professional fields and in the liberal arts. Activities that bring diverse groups of students together can be especially valuable for supporting liberal learning, especially when the program addresses directly some of liberal education's classic content themes and central modes of thinking. One example is a national competition called the Intercollegiate Ethics Bowl, which brings together campus teams from across the country to deliberate about ethical questions. In advance of the competition, campus teams receive cases that pose ethical dilemmas and develop approaches to resolving the moral problems raised in the cases. During the competition, judges ask searching questions about one of the cases and teams advance based on how well they are able to answer the questions. Successful teams move from local to regional to national competitions. Clearly, this kind of extended immersion in ethical concerns can not only build intellectual capacities for dealing with complex ethical questions but also makes ethical questions more salient in the perceptions and worldviews of participating students. Business students who take part in this kind of activity can then bring their deepened ethical sensibilities to their coursework and, eventually, to their careers.

Campus Culture

We were impressed at several programs we visited by the power of the larger campus culture to support a shared sense of purpose around liberal education. Morehouse College, Santa Clara University, and Portland

State University all have strong and distinctive cultures in this regard. Building on their particular mission, history, and setting, each has a culture that ties together students in different departments, providing a common language and some degree of shared outlook.

Morehouse College's mission of educating black men makes it unique in American higher education and gives it a distinctive ethos of brotherhood, solidarity, and social purpose. The legacy of alumnus Martin Luther King Jr. permeates the institution, serving as a focal point for a commitment to social justice and service to moral ideals. Students see themselves as walking in the light cast by King and other Morehouse graduates who were leaders in the civil rights movement. In this spirit, ethical leadership is stressed in both the business and the arts and sciences divisions. By design, an ambitious Leadership Center is located in the business division's new building as is the Bonner Center for Community Service—though both serve all departments in the college.

Morehouse also has a strong culture of mutual respect that affects relationships between faculty and students, attitudes toward the central administration, students' manners, and even their dress. In the words of the president, Robert Franklin, Morehouse students should aspire to be "Renaissance men," which he interprets as broadly cultured, cosmopolitan, and ethically high minded. In Franklin's view, the term connects as directly with the Harlem Renaissance as it does with European traditions.

At least as important, administrators, faculty, and students at Morehouse hold and aspire to a shared image of "the educated person," which includes broad knowledge in the arts and sciences as well as professional accomplishment and social contribution. This shared understanding of what it means to be an educated person is a strong force for interweaving knowledge and intellectual skills with the exploration of meaning and for integrating liberal and business education. Because social contribution is so central to the institution's understanding of what it means to be an educated person, a Morehouse business education naturally addresses questions of social impact and significance as well as profitability.

In our 2003 book, *Educating Citizens,* we spell out a number of elements that go into making a strong culture of social concern and purpose in college. These elements include physical symbols and other features of the campus landscape that serve as reminders of the institution's ideals or facilitate communication about them. At Morehouse, for example, a large statue of Martin Luther King Jr. occupies a prominent place on campus. Iconic stories that are told over and over contribute to identification with the institution and to a shared vision of the self as a member of the institutional community—a "Morehouse man," as we heard many times during our visit. Rituals marking transitions, achievements, and other significant moments can also be powerful carriers of culture and that is true at Morehouse.

Santa Clara University shares the Morehouse commitment to social justice, though at Santa Clara that commitment is rooted in Jesuit Catholic traditions. Competence, conscience, and compassion are the "three Cs" that students across the campus recognize as a hallmark of the university and its educational ideals. We were struck by the extent to which administrative leaders of the university, especially then-president Paul Locatelli, speak and act in ways that infuse the campus culture with a Jesuit sense of social justice.

This perspective clearly permeates education for business and other professions as well as liberal arts. As Father Locatelli told us, "The focus of liberal education should be humanistic—the world and our relation to it, developing a person who can serve society with knowledge, judgment, and virtue as an integrated whole. In regard to business education, this humanistic ideal is just as important." Not surprisingly, then, he insisted that a purely economic model of business, which understands the field to be directed primarily toward creating economic value for business owners (and presumably for the self as well), is inadequate. Careers in business, as in other fields, must instead be driven by a sense of calling, which includes the desire to contribute to the welfare of the world in a larger sense.

We were impressed that there seems to be no question in the minds of students, faculty, and administrators that Santa Clara is a liberal arts institution, despite the fact that it has a number of professional schools and that business is the most popular undergraduate major. For the most part, students and faculty we talked to define liberal learning as going beyond instrumentally useful skills to include a deeper understanding of the world and a commitment to making a positive contribution. As at Morehouse, we discovered a shared sense of the educated person at Santa Clara, which strengthens the ties between the liberal arts and vocational fields such as business.

Portland State University (PSU) is a public institution and it was no surprise to us that the campus culture there is quite different from those of Morehouse and Santa Clara. At the same time, there are two key dimensions of the Portland State culture that reflect the same sense of shared purpose and concern for others that we saw at Morehouse and Santa Clara. First, PSU prides itself on being an integral part of the greater Portland region. Most of the students come from that region and expect to live there after graduation. The university is situated in the middle of Portland and a bridge linking two of its buildings prominently proclaims, "Let Knowledge Serve the City." From the moment students consider applying to Portland State and receive materials about the university, they are reminded that it is a great urban resource for the betterment of the community.

This community focus is reflected in many aspects of the curriculum. For example, senior capstone courses in the university's innovative general education curriculum are designed to provide students with the opportunity to apply what they have learned to a real challenge faced by the metropolitan community. The commitment to community is also apparent in the cocurriculum. Many student organizations involve service to and connections with the local community.

In addition to being integrally connected with the Portland community, the university emphasizes environmental sustainability in many aspects of its activities and this theme also infuses its entire culture. "Green, it's not just our school color" is a frequent tag line seen on the campus. This orientation toward environmental sustainability provides important common ground between business education and the liberal arts. Environmental concerns reflect civic values and reach into multiple dimensions of business and its interactions with society.

Morehouse College, Santa Clara University, and Portland State University illustrate three quite different ways to embody the values of a liberal education in the culture of a college or university. Their particular features cannot be exactly replicated at other campuses but attention to the different kinds of cultural embodiment these campuses exhibit can guide other institutions in their efforts to develop institutional cultures that inspire people and draw them together. Of course, there are many, often conflicting, strands in the culture of any complex institution. And culture is not static or objectively given. We cannot know what students or faculty make of particular cultural rituals or artifacts unless we observe and listen to them. But there are clearly steps that institutions can take to bring the values of a liberal education to the center of the culture and we have seen many in our research over the years that succeed in doing this.

O

The key to creating a successfully integrated undergraduate education is institutional intentionality. Integration is a complex process and it does not take hold at a deep level without conscious design, cultivation, and commitment. Individual students and faculty must see and embrace the value of making connections between business and larger liberal learning goals, and curriculum, cocurriculum, and campus culture must reflect and enact that value.

Fortunately, as the examples set forth in this chapter make clear, there are many roads to this destination. What works in one place cannot simply be transplanted into another. But having diverse examples in view gives a concrete feel for the range of possible strategies and can, we hope, stimulate creativity and innovation as campuses learn from one another's practices. In Chapter Eight, we turn to two topics that are ripe sites for just this kind of exchange and learning across diverse settings: globalization and entrepreneurship.

8

EMERGING AGENDAS

GLOBALIZATION AND ENTREPRENEURSHIP

WE HAVE TALKED in previous chapters about the importance of curricular structures and pedagogical strategies that can integrate liberal and business learning. Less has been said about the liberal arts *content* of that learning. It is clear, though, that if students are to make sense of the world and their place in it as well as prepare for a career, they need broad knowledge of many fields in the arts and sciences. Allowing for considerable flexibility in that content makes sense but science, social science, history, literature, and the arts all play key roles in understanding the world.

Knowledge of these disciplines is valuable for its own sake and engaging them with an explorer mentality helps create a lively, fascinated intelligence that drives the pursuit of understanding throughout life. Our central focus in this book is the value of liberal learning for careers in business, and this chapter attempts to show why and how the content of liberal learning is critical in preparing students to grapple with the challenges business presents. To do so, we will focus on two issues that are perennial but especially acute in the moment: globalization and entrepreneurship or innovation. These are only two among a larger set of urgent, complex challenges that require insights from many disciplines, but we hope they will provide compelling examples of our larger argument about integrating liberal arts content with preparation for business—and a useful contrast as well. In the case of globalization, a significant degree of integration is already in place; in the case of entrepreneurship, connections are only now beginning to emerge but the potential for integration is significant. Both offer lessons about what it takes to cultivate meaningful connections.

Education for a Globally Connected World

Over the past decade or so there has been a heightened recognition of the globally interconnected nature of business and the ways that globalization has intensified and complicated competitive currents of contemporary business. This heightened awareness also reveals the ways that strategic competition intersects with the social and environmental effects of business. The escalating effects of globalization represent a major shift in the business environment, and the result is a pervasive sense of threat as well as excitement and opportunity.

Business educators are well aware of this shift and make serious efforts to prepare students to deal with it. In fact, undergraduate education as a whole has begun to acknowledge preparation for a global world as an important learning goal (Association of American Colleges and Universities, 2007; Hovland, 2009). Achieving this goal requires students to adopt a broader sociogeographic perspective that taps into economic, political, and cultural forms of pluralism. The shared recognition of this complex aim represents important common ground for liberal learning and business and is an area in which business educators have a lot to offer higher education more generally. And because the issues connected with globalization require the perspectives of many disciplines and stimulate interest and concern across the academy, globalization is an ideal context for integrating business and liberal education.

Global cultural literacy opens connections among the full array of disciplines, including the social sciences, history, literature and language, the arts, religion, science, mathematics, and technology. It also opens opportunities for exercising the three modes of thinking we have identified with liberal learning. For starters, making sense of the complexity of global business naturally draws on and builds students' Analytical Thinking. Education for global perspective also requires and helps to develop Multiple Framing and the Reflective Exploration of Meaning. In fact, deep learning about cultures other than one's own is a quintessential arena in which young people become aware of the partial and contingent nature of their own previously unquestioned assumptions and perspectives. High-quality courses and programs that induct students into a global perspective help them see that arrangements they have taken for granted are not "given by nature" but instead represent one possibility among an array of quite different options, some of which may be equally good or even better. This understanding gives students fresh eyes for looking at their own culture and a better sense of what it means to be acculturated: that no one is culture-free and that everyone operates within particular, though multifaceted and complex, cultural systems.

This kind of learning means more than seeing other cultures as different and exotic, though at first the customs of another culture may seem strange or amusing. The challenge is to help students begin to see the world from others' points of view. In order for this to happen, students need to experience cultural differences from a decentered perspective and grasp, on an experiential and emotional level, that there is more than one legitimate way to make sense of and assign value to human arrangements.

Not all of the courses on international business that we observed provide experience in seeing the world from multiple perspectives; some maintain what amounts to a U.S. point of view. When the latter is true, students are asked to learn about norms and preferences elsewhere in order to increase their chances for commercial success in international settings or when working with international partners. These types of courses acknowledge the risk of inadvertently violating the norms of non-U.S. settings or partners and help students avoid the consequences that arise from such violations, but this approach provides only a shallow grasp of different cultural perspectives.

During our campus visits, however, we observed courses designed to teach for much deeper forms of global awareness and to instill an appreciation of the rich and profoundly diverse cultural contexts of different nations, regions, and ethnic or religious groups. Some offer sophisticated analyses of the intersecting cultural influences of a region's history, religious traditions, arts, political systems, geography, and the like. Courses aimed at this kind of understanding take diverse cultural perspectives seriously and provide deeper and more thoughtful engagement with the complexities and subtleties of international collaborations and globally connected economies. Many of these courses and programs draw directly on the humanities and social sciences to give students a more textured understanding of another region or of issues that are approached very differently by other countries.

Globalization and the Culture of Business in East Asia, offered by Indiana University's Liberal Arts and Management Program, illustrates how such a course can work. It explores the post–World War II emergence of east Asia as a locus of economic, technological, and cultural dynamism, taking a historical perspective on the economies of east Asia and drawing centrally from texts written by Chinese and Japanese authors.

Questions addressed in the course include the following: what historical developments influence the contemporary shape of east Asian state systems, how do these systems differ, and how are the various economies unified by goals, policies, and orientation to the larger global system? What were the effects of Japanese imperialism between 1900 and 1945 on shaping the political economy of the empire, including Taiwan and Korea? What cultural systems and core values underlie contemporary east Asian business practices? How did U.S. business first ignore, then contest, and finally accept these practices within its own business models? How does an understanding of east Asian capitalism help us anticipate the future of globalization more broadly?

As students consider these questions, they learn about how capitalism varies when it is embedded in different political and cultural systems and think through the very different assumptions that form the foundations of those systems. Clearly, this course is not just a set of tips about things to watch out for when marketing products or hiring workers abroad.

Ethical Considerations

As students move toward a greater appreciation of the deep diversity of world cultures and attempt to extend generous interpretations to unfamiliar ways, many lose their grip on any overarching set of principles by which they might make sound judgments. The result is sometimes a bad case of cultural relativism. Yet, as world citizens and as business people working in a global context, they will need to make decisions and often those decisions will need to take into account *conflicting* (not just interestingly different) moral norms. The third mode of liberal learning, the Reflective Exploration of Meaning, is needed to help students find ways to respect others' points of view while also finding some firm principles that can guide their own commitments and actions.

A course on corporate responsibility at the University of Pennsylvania's Wharton School illustrates what is possible in this regard. The class session we observed focused on gender equity in an international context. Among other things, students in the class role-play a case concerning a U.S. company that has an office in Latin America. A male student from Latin America played the senior manager in the case and a woman played his number two. In the case the woman is more knowledgeable about the business deal in question than is the male senior manager—but he excludes his more knowledgeable colleague from the discussion with local clients. She is understandably upset but the senior manager defends his behavior by invoking local cultural expectations.

In the role-play, the male manager says that, given the context, he does not feel free to follow his own personal inclination toward gender equality. The woman says that she is torn; she recognizes her colleague's difficult position but also feels that she is not being given a chance to succeed. Another student suggests that she should adapt to the work setting, wielding power the way women in that culture do—by acting in a subordinate manner while attempting to control the situation indirectly. Yet another student argues that the woman should confront her colleague, asking him to give her a chance by treating her more equally. At the end of the role-play, the professor sums up: "I think most of us agree that you have to recognize and respect cultural differences. Another point I think most of us would agree on is that Sarah should have been told a lot more than she was. Another thing that occurred to me is that we often have to be creative about these situations. The experience I've had with many executives in this kind of case is that they say, 'We didn't think we could put a woman in the Middle East, but we did, and she's been tremendously successful.'"

The Place of Global Learning in the Curriculum

All of the business schools we visited offer undergraduate courses that directly address international business, international economics, regional issues relating to business, and the various sources and effects of globalization. Many of these courses address the complex issues raised by today's globally interconnected economic system as well, including trade policy, foreign exchange and international finance, regional and global financial crises, and the implications of state action for market efficiency. Other courses, such as Indiana University's Globalization and the Culture of Business in East Asia, address the cultural contexts of especially critical regions. Another common focus is business functions such as communications or marketing that raise special challenges in a global context.

Some schools go beyond individual courses and offer more comprehensive programs that allow students to pursue international issues in greater depth. The Global Perspectives track is a popular choice among students completing the Liberal Studies Major (LSM) at Bentley University, for example. These students put together a set of courses from arts and sciences and from business that examine international issues of interest to them. Most who choose this option have developed a strong interest in particular countries or regions and have learned the languages and spent time studying abroad. They are enthusiastic about the LSM program, talking about having their eyes opened, growing as a person, becoming more open-minded—and about learning lessons directly relevant to their careers in business. Bentley also offers a Global Studies Major, which requires a strong language component and a semester abroad.

The Wharton School's Huntsman Program in International Studies and Business is particularly ambitious. Students enter this four-year program as freshmen, earning a BA in International Studies from the University of Pennsylvania's School of Arts and Sciences and a BS in economics from the Wharton School. The integrated curriculum coordinates extensive coursework in the liberal arts, advanced language, and business and includes a required study abroad experience. Huntsman students must become fluent in a second language and specialize in an area of the world in which that language is spoken.

In-depth programs such as these reach students who want special preparation for global business, but it is also important to reach those who do not seek that preparation. For this reason, global issues should be integrated into courses on a wide range of topics, and this is a trend we saw reflected in our campus visits. A senior management professor at Morehouse College, for example, told us that the biggest change in management textbooks since the 1990s is their greatly increased emphasis on international issues; the book he uses for the required basic management course includes a chapter specifically addressing international issues, and international examples are prominent in all of the other chapters. Cultural diversity within U.S. workplaces is also receiving increased attention in this and other management courses and textbooks.

Our observations of courses in management and other disciplines confirm this professor's perception. For example, Wharton's Corporate Responsibility is not a course in global learning per se, yet it frequently engages students in thinking through how they will deal with cultural conflicts they may encounter if they work abroad or collaborate with colleagues in other countries and how to think about business decisions with global implications such as outsourcing.

Foreign language courses are another natural place for integrating intercultural learning, although not all language courses take advantage of this potential. Bentley University has a strong emphasis on preparation for global business and its Center for Languages and International Collaboration plays an important role in that preparation, offering resources that include real-time satellite broadcasting of international news, a global theater equipped for videoconferencing with universities abroad, a multilingual jukebox, and a large collection of international periodicals and other publications.

Study Abroad

One of the most familiar ways to educate for global perspectives and intercultural learning is through study abroad programs. These include short-term experiences lasting between one and eight weeks, a semester or more at a satellite campus of the students' home university, or a semester or more at a foreign university. The number of college students studying abroad has more than tripled since the mid-1990s, although the overall percentage of college student participation has remained steady as access to higher education among less affluent students has expanded (Lewin, 2009). Not surprisingly, participation rates vary significantly from one institution to another, depending on the school's emphasis on international issues and on the financial resources available to the typical student. Nationally, short-term programs have higher participation rates than programs that extend for a semester or longer.

Study abroad programs vary significantly in the degree to which they structure students' experiences in order to foster global and intercultural learning. Unfortunately, some students treat study abroad more as tourist opportunities than as preparation for global citizenship and international career trajectories. A recent journal article on global learning by the director of study abroad at a major U.S. university notes, "Many [students] still see study abroad as a semester off, a break from the . . . demands of higher education" (Lewin, 2009, p. 8). "We find ourselves pushing these loftier goals onto students against their primary expectations for travel, adventure, and pleasure-seeking" (p. 9). Furthermore, the vast majority of students choose to spend their semesters abroad in affluent European countries, thereby limiting their exposure to cultures that are the most different from that of the United States.

In the face of these realities, study abroad programs are most powerful when they are intentional about goals, providing structured ways for students to learn about their host country's culture, history, geography, and politics and to deepen their knowledge and engagement after they return. An institutional commitment to teach global systems, area studies, and languages provides a rich context of preparation for students who study abroad and for the many who do not. Faculty-led short-term international experiences and experiences on satellite campuses may not provide the same degree of immersion as a semester in a foreign university but more closely supervised programs provide more control over the quality of students' learning experiences.

All of our site visit schools sponsor both short-term and semester- or year-long programs that serve undergraduate business students. In contrast to the sometimes frivolous image of study abroad experiences, our impression was that participating students are strongly motivated to learn and to build international connections, perhaps because the effects of globalization are salient and opportunities abound for careers with an international dimension. This productive use of shorter- and longer-term study abroad offerings is an area in which business faculty can be a resource to the campus more broadly.

Some study abroad experiences for business students are embedded in programs that extend for several years. We have already mentioned Wharton's Huntsman Program and Bentley's Global Studies Major. Similarly, students at NYU's Stern School have the option of choosing the World Studies track or the Business and Political Economy major, both of which integrate international experiences with coursework. Students in the World Studies track spend a semester in London, a semester in Shanghai, and a shorter period in Latin America. Students who choose the Business and Political Economy major spend two semesters in London and one in Shanghai.

In addition to providing in-depth experience for a wide swath of interested students, a few institutions ensure that *all* business majors go abroad, at least for a short-term program. At the Stern School, for example, all junior-year students spend a week visiting a company in another country, with each section of the course connecting with a different company. Students learn about the opportunities and challenges the company is facing and then create recommendations to help improve its performance. Project reports must address macroeconomic, political, sociological, and business strategy questions and often include recommendations about the company's social impact as well as sales and profitability. The development of these project reports is structured as a competition with a single group as the winner.

The Stern faculty believe that this and other international experiences have a strong impact on their students. Many students refer to their international experiences in their regular courses, describing things they saw in China or Italy, for example, and asking instructors to deal with international dimensions of the topic. Economic inequalities around the world become more vivid for students who have studied in developing countries. Severe poverty and extreme income inequalities, which can seem abstract or remote when addressed in the classroom, become very real when students experience them face to face. Similarly, a study abroad experience in Germany that compares German and American health care systems leads to better understanding of health care policy questions in the United States and abroad.

Cocurricular Activities with an International Dimension

In Chapter Seven, we discuss the importance of students' cocurricular activities as a source of integration and liberal learning. Popular activities for business students include discipline-based and other business-oriented clubs, service and service-learning experiences, residence hall programs, and campus events such as invited speakers. Each of these areas can incorporate an international dimension. Wharton's Huntsman Program, for example, includes a residence hall component in which students live and participate together in a number of residency-based activities. Santa Clara, which places strong emphasis on service and service-learning experiences, provides many opportunities for service trips abroad during summers and spring breaks and business students are well represented in these programs.

Another way to internationalize cocurricular opportunities is through speaker series, typically open to the entire campus community, featuring international as well as U.S. experts on issues of global economics and business as well as geopolitical issues. Morehouse College, for example, sponsors an ongoing program in which elected presidents of African countries come to campus to talk about leadership and about issues facing their countries. Some business faculty provide course credit for attendance at the lectures.

Some of the clubs that business students participate in also have an international dimension. One of the most prominent is Students in Free Enterprise (SIFE). As the organization's Web site describes it (http://www.sife.org/aboutsife/Pages/Overview.aspx), SIFE's mission is to "create a better, more sustainable world through the positive power of business" (Students in Free Enterprise, 2010). The organization lists fifteen hundred member universities in forty countries. SIFE's programs include national and international community-service projects along with an annual competition in which student teams present the results of their projects. Each year, the competition yields regional and national winners as well as the SIFE World Cup.

In addition to the wide array of cocurricular activities with international dimensions, the majority of undergraduate business programs enroll significant numbers of international students. Some schools sponsor formal exchange programs that recruit students from particular countries and many simply attract large numbers of students from abroad. Either way, the result is a multinational campus community. Although this can lead to tensions when norms about gender roles, class divisions, and other highly charged issues collide, it also plays an important part in preparing students to live and work in a globally connected world.

Entrepreneurship and Innovation

The development of new businesses is widely acknowledged as a key factor in maintaining a vibrant economy, and entrepreneurial efforts in corporate settings often play a critical role in the survival and growth of established businesses. The closely related issue of innovation is also critical for the future of U.S. business. Despite the evident importance of this theme in today's world, entrepreneurship is not strongly represented in the curricula of most undergraduate business programs nor is it widespread in relevant areas in the arts and sciences. The relative paucity of offerings in this area is in striking contrast to the wealth of opportunities for learning to function effectively in a globally connected world. Whereas every business school and department we saw acknowledges that learning about globalization is essential to preparation for business careers, only a few, such as Babson College, specialize in preparing students for entrepreneurship, with most content to treat the subject as a niche issue, providing only modest coverage. And because issues relating to entrepreneurship and innovation are seldom addressed in a serious way in courses on other topics, and courses on entrepreneurship are seldom required, it is easy for students to miss these experiences entirely. The question, then, is what would it take to cultivate the level of integration that characterizes globalization within the emerging area of entrepreneurship? How might the topic be reframed to provide opportunities to find and forge connections with liberal arts disciplines, and what are the benefits that would follow for business students as they prepare for work and life?

A Broad View of Entrepreneurship

Although entrepreneurship is often associated with the establishment of new ventures, both scholars and educators in the field define the term more broadly. Donald F. Kuratko, the founder and director of Indiana University's Entrepreneurship Program, told us that he thinks of entrepreneurship as "a way of thinking. It is the ability to see opportunity in confusing situations, the capacity to approach problems with innovation and creativity and to apply talent and abilities in new ways." Patricia Greene, F. W. Olin Distinguished Chair of Entrepreneurship and former Provost of Babson College, also talked about entrepreneurship in terms that include but go beyond new ventures: "Entrepreneurship involves the ability to identify opportunities, mobilize resources, and provide leadership to create something of value." This creation of value may take place through the establishment of new businesses or through revitalization of mature organizations in response to a perceived opportunity. In this sense, an expansive conception of entrepreneurship has important cultural, governance, and systems-design implications for how organizations are structured.

As with globalization, the arts and sciences have a great deal to contribute to entrepreneurship, which is therefore an ideal site for integrating liberal and business education. For starters, it can broaden what social psychologists call a *social cognitive and systems perspective,* helping students move out of rote status quo thinking into more integrative, change-oriented thinking. In this sense, as Kuratko pointed out, entrepreneurship is closely connected with innovation, which may involve new products, new production methods, new markets, or new forms of organization. This relatively broad conception of entrepreneurship seems to open the way for entrepreneurial thinking and skill to be included as goals in courses on a wide range of topics, not only those that directly address the creation of new ventures. A broader view of entrepreneurship, along with a fuller recognition of its intrinsic connections with innovation, also points to the (as yet largely unrealized) potential for enriching the teaching of entrepreneurship by drawing on the insights and content of liberal arts disciplines.

Social Entrepreneurship, Social Impact, and Sustainability

In recent years, the concept of entrepreneurship has been extended to ventures that use business practices and disciplines to create innovative solutions to intractable social problems through what has come to be known as *social entrepreneurship.* Social ventures are most likely to be not-for-profit organizations but some are businesses that make a profit. In order to be considered a social entrepreneurship venture rather than a socially responsible business, the social mission must be front and center. But it is worth noting that social entrepreneurship anchors the end of a continuum defined by the relative centrality of social impact and its contribution to the mission and operations of the institution. From this perspective, social entrepreneurship can be understood as an instance of a wider set of emerging concerns that include (in what has been called "the triple bottom line") social impact, sustainability, and stakeholder theory—all of which entail a thoroughgoing emphasis on social impact over the longer term, including consideration of how business decisions affect future generations.

In recent decades, social entrepreneurship as a conceptual and organizational approach has become quite influential as a way of thinking about the organized pursuit of social change; it is now playing an increasingly central role within contemporary philanthropy and other nonprofit activities. Several organizations—including prominently Ashoka: Innovators for the Public and the Skoll Foundation—have led this movement. As interest grows, social entrepreneurship seems to offer a valuable way to channel college students' idealism while also teaching a wide array of organizational and leadership capacities. Whether social enterprises use a for-profit or nonprofit model, they share many functions and organizational structures with profit-centered businesses, so many of the efforts to prepare students for entrepreneurship apply to social entrepreneurship as well. Programs to support social entrepreneurship can also contribute to students' capacity to become business entrepreneurs.

In order to succeed in social ventures, students need practical skills, the kind of expanded vision that feeds innovation and a sense of purpose and passion. To minimize the inadvertent harm that often results from well-intentioned efforts to intervene in the status quo—particularly in cultural contexts other than one's own—students also need a working knowledge of the complexity of public response to interventions, an understanding of the history of social movements, and a grasp of the social, institutional, legal, policy, and other contexts in which their efforts will play out. In this sense, too, preparation for social entrepreneurship specifically is closely linked with preparation for socially responsible, sustainable enterprise more generally.

Unfortunately, courses on social entrepreneurship are even less common in undergraduate business programs than business-oriented entrepreneurship courses. And this is a significant missed opportunity—one that could help students learn to apply and integrate the business disciplines with liberal learning content and modes of thought while also engaging their motivation to make a positive difference in the world. This attention to social contribution would be a valuable counterweight to the intensely profit-focused education most business students receive.

In addition, business entrepreneurship and social entrepreneurship provide opportunities for students to explore unique, self-created integrations of disparate subject matters. Some students may be especially interested in entrepreneurial activities in the arts or education, for example, or in topics such as the history of gender or race in new venture creation. The Kauffman Foundation's ambitious programs of entrepreneurship education for students in the arts and sciences generate exactly these kinds of imaginative intersections.

An important caveat is raised with the application of the principles of entrepreneurship and business models to education, philanthropy, the arts, and other domains outside the purview of conventional business. We talked in earlier chapters about the different institutional logics that characterize different domains, arguing that one of the great benefits of liberal learning for business students is to help them understand business as one institution among many and appreciate the range of qualitatively different logics governing different kinds of institutions. If this is achieved, it should heighten awareness of the times when an institutional logic from one domain, usually business, is being applied to another domain, say education. This heightened awareness makes it possible to ask how, precisely, the business perspective can benefit the educational domain and also what its risks are. Entrepreneurship education in the arts, education, philanthropy, and social enterprise more generally could make an important contribution by raising these issues with students. Instead of allowing students to think that "everything is business," these programs could encourage them to reflect carefully on the implications of that commonly held assumption. Helping students develop a more sophisticated grasp of the complex relationships among social institutions and their varied institutional logics can be an important antidote to the unthinking application of business principles to issues that are not always well served by the wholesale extension of those principles.

Why Entrepreneurship Gets Short Shrift

A number of reasons for the relative neglect of both business entrepreneurship and social entrepreneurship emerged from our conversations with business faculty and administrators. Despite significant student interest in new business development, many business educators think that recent graduates are not seasoned enough to become successful entrepreneurs and they want to discourage unrealistic and risky aspirations. This belief may help explain the greater focus on entrepreneurship in graduate than undergraduate business education.

In addition, some faculty and administrators we talked to explained that entrepreneurship is deemphasized because it is not a recognized business discipline. This means that tenure-track faculty teaching entrepreneurship courses are likely operating outside their area of specialization or (more often) that these courses are not taught by academics but by successful entrepreneurs who bring a very practical orientation. In either case, entrepreneurship's relatively weak ties to a recognized discipline or body of theory diminish the field's place in the academic hierarchy. As in arts and sciences disciplines, the values of the academy—including abstraction, analytic rigor, and a focus on theory—are strong in every field of professional preparation we have investigated, including law, medicine, engineering, theology, school teaching, and nursing. In all of these, prestige and legitimacy are closely linked with the degree to which the field is understood as fundamentally academic in nature.

The widespread perception that entrepreneurship is not a serious academic field is reflected in publishing patterns as well. Busenitz, West, Shepherd, Nelson, Chandler, and Zacharakis (2003), for example, found that only 2 percent of the articles published in major management journals focused on entrepreneurship and only a small proportion of those addressed entrepreneurship *theory*. In addition, articles on entrepreneurship are more likely to cite major management journals than to refer to entrepreneurship journals. This is beginning to shift, however, and Busenitz's analysis points to the increasing prominence of several journals dedicated to entrepreneurship research and theory, such as the *Journal of Business Venturing*. At this point, entrepreneurship seems to be an emerging discipline, but it has a long way to go if it is to reach the level of emphasis in business education that the core business disciplines enjoy.

Current Approaches to Teaching Entrepreneurship and Social Entrepreneurship

This is not to say that entrepreneurship is entirely neglected, even at schools that do not specialize in this area. All of our site visit schools offer at least two courses on entrepreneurship, although almost always as electives. This is consistent with national data. In a review of entrepreneurship education programs in the United States, Katz (2006) notes that most programs include two core courses. One is an introduction to entrepreneurship, which typically involves the application of the core business disciplines to small or new businesses. The second focuses on the creation of business plans, sometimes with competitions judged by outsiders.

Some of the entrepreneurship courses we saw are notable for employing pedagogies of enactment (see Chapter Six). We have already described Foundations of Management and Entrepreneurship, the signature first-year course at Babson College—an institution with an international reputation for entrepreneurship education. FME students actually start new businesses during their freshman year, in the process learning a great deal about the functional areas of business and their interconnected nature.

Babson also offers a more advanced course called Entrepreneurship and New Ventures, in which students design a new venture and create a business plan for it, though they stop short of implementing the plan. In the process, they conduct research on the field of the proposed venture: the competition, the technologies involved, the market environment, and other issues that could affect the venture's success. Students do this research in teams, each taking a different role in what amounts to a simulation of the early stages of new venture development.

In our visit to this course, we observed midterm presentations in which student teams presented their assessments of the strength of their identified opportunity at that point, its potential risks, next steps, and factors that needed further review. The instructor urged teams to look closely at the risks: "Don't brush risks under the rug. Bring them out and address them." As students made their presentations, other class members acted as potential investors, pressing to uncover information they would need to know in order to evaluate the opportunity presented. In the process, the instructor tied the issues and questions they raised to explications of strategy, organizational structure, competitor analysis, intellectual property and technology issues, implementation questions, and the like.

Although our site visits did not uncover much direct preparation for social entrepreneurship, we did see some courses in which students learn to apply business principles and skills to social problems such as poverty and environmental sustainability. These efforts parallel those for business entrepreneurship and include courses in which students create business plans for new social ventures and courses that apply the basic business disciplines to nonprofit organizations. Some of these courses teach students to apply business practices to social problems or nonprofit organizations by engaging them with community organizations through service learning in underserved communities or in organizations with specifically social missions. For example, in Portland State University's senior capstone course Marketing for Non-Profit Organizations, students work with a community partner, Idealist.org, to create a marketing plan that will increase the organization's capacity to meet its goals. (Idealist.org is a Web-based organization that brings nonprofits working for social change together with individuals seeking jobs or volunteer opportunities in that sector.)

Courses that address entrepreneurship and social entrepreneurship through these kinds of pedagogies of enactment are important learning opportunities even for students who plan to work in corporate settings. They provide hands-on experience applying knowledge from the core business disciplines and, in the process, help students experience the integrated nature of that knowledge in practice. They also help students learn to work together effectively in teams. Based on these courses alone, however, it is difficult to see how entrepreneurial thinking could be threaded productively throughout the curriculum, as preparation for globalization is beginning to be. Nor does this approach give significant attention to the less tangible dimensions of entrepreneurial effectiveness, most especially innovation or creativity.

Greater emphasis on innovation would not only strengthen the preparation of students who wish to pursue new ventures or corporate entrepreneurship, but it would also help make entrepreneurship a more pervasive presence throughout the undergraduate curriculum. At this point, however, entrepreneurship education as we observed it does not fully recognize and take advantage of larger themes such as innovation and creative thinking, the development of fresh but grounded visions of future directions, and responsiveness to a constantly changing environment. Likewise, a fuller recognition that social entrepreneurship reflects and connects with the broader themes of social impact, consideration of the perspectives of multiple stakeholders, and various dimensions of sustainability could pave the way for integrating these important foundations of social entrepreneurship into a wider array of courses in ways that draw on content areas both within and beyond business.

Entrepreneurial Thinking as Liberal Learning

Whether it involves new ventures or revitalization of existing organizations, entrepreneurship is widely recognized as involving several stages, beginning with opportunity recognition and assessment and moving to early implementation and then to further development, usually in highly competitive contexts. Especially in the initial stage, successful entrepreneurs have to see potential opportunities where others do not and they must continually assess and adapt to an ever-shifting environment as the venture develops. Because that environment includes changing dynamics within the organization as well as shifts in external forces, entrepreneurs face considerable information overload and ambiguity and must often make consequential decisions in the face of substantial uncertainty. To operate effectively in this kind of situation, they must be able to extract critical variables from a noisy background.

To understand what it takes to negotiate these many challenges, recent research has focused on the cognitive dimensions of entrepreneurship, looking at whether people who are particularly good at identifying and responding to opportunities think differently than others. One influential strand of this research focuses on the mental models or cognitive schemas that represent an individual's knowledge and beliefs about how the world and its various domains work—for example, a successful entrepreneur's expert grasp of multiple critical forces driving the market environment and the relational dynamics among those forces (Gaglio & Katz, 2001; West, 2007).

A well-developed field of research on expertise in many domains has shown that the cognitive schemas that underlie expert performance are more richly elaborated, more highly organized, and more fully cross-linked with schemas in related domains than are those of novices. Research and theory that bring this cognitive expertise framework to entrepreneurship contrast with earlier research on the topic, which tended to focus on relatively fixed personality traits that were thought to characterize successful entrepreneurs.

Most notably for our argument in this book, Gaglio and Katz (2001) have identified a number of critical features of the "alert" entrepreneur that resonate strongly with the dimensions of liberal learning. In their view, alert individuals come to their more expert modes of framing because when they notice apparent anomalies—things that their current mode of thinking cannot explain—they seek to understand what is really going on rather than continuing to rely on existing schemas that cannot account for the new information. Nonalert individuals, by contrast, may notice discrepant information or signals of change but remain entrenched in current schemas; thus the cognitive status quo is maintained. As a result, alert individuals develop more highly attuned mental models that allow them to become aware of patterns that are not apparent to others. As Gaglio and Katz put it, "Alert individuals, then, take to heart and have integrated into their schema the graduate student mantra: 'What are three other ways to think about this?'" (p. 101). Over time, a consistent habit of thinking more flexibly and creatively contributes to and is supported by richer, more elaborate, more coherent representations of the market environment, including historical, sociopolitical, and cultural phenomena. This conception of entrepreneurial or innovative expertise points to a need for education that goes beyond the core business disciplines and technical skills, highlighting the importance of the kind of contextual knowledge carried by arts and sciences disciplines. So, for example, a rich contextual understanding could prompt entrepreneurs to notice relevant trends such as demographic shifts and make them more thoughtful about the ways that demographic patterns relate to other social and technological changes. This kind of thinking may be what Peter Drucker (1985) had in mind when he proposed that entrepreneurial management is, in essence, a liberal art, drawing on lessons from history, sociology, psychology, philosophy, culture, and religion.

In addition, entrepreneurial thinking appears to benefit from the intellectual capacity for and inclination toward what we have called Multiple Framing as well as Analytical Thinking. That is, alert individuals do not experience their cognitive schemes as literal representations of objective reality but as conceptual models based on working assumptions that are open to adaptation or revision to make better sense of experiences that do not fit the current model.

The Opposable Mind: Integrative Thinking

We have already discussed the work of Roger Martin. His study of successful business leaders (2007) resonates with Gaglio and Katz's description of entrepreneurial alertness: "The leaders I have studied share at least one trait, aside from their talent for innovation and long-term business success," Martin writes. "They have the predisposition and the capacity to hold two diametrically opposing ideas in their heads. And then, without panicking or settling for one alternative or the other, they're able to produce a synthesis that is superior to either opposing idea" (p. 6). In Gaglio and Katz's terms, they develop a new, more complex, and comprehensive mental model. For Martin, the capacity to achieve this kind of synthesis constitutes "integrative thinking," which he considers "the hallmark of exceptional businesses and the people who run them" (p. 6). Martin suggests that integrative thinking reveals an "opposable mind," able to hold two conflicting ideas in constructive tension and use that tension to create a new and superior idea, just as human beings' opposable thumb makes it possible for them to perform difficult manual tasks (p. 7).

Martin's account of integrative thinking includes some of the same qualities that characterize the best entrepreneurial thinking and, not coincidentally, the features of liberal learning we advocate in this book. Those with "opposable minds" habitually distinguish conceptual models from the reality they are meant to represent, and this capacity is, in Martin's view, critical in helping them find creative resolutions of apparently incommensurable perspectives. Additionally, similar to those characterized by entrepreneurial alertness, Martin's integrative thinkers take a broad view of what factors may be relevant to important decisions. They "welcome the mess," realizing that the best answers often arise from complexity (p. 41). They are skilled in seeing patterns, connections, and causal relationships, keeping the entire problem in mind while working on its individual parts. And the causal relationships they discern are likely to be multidirectional and nonlinear. Conventional thinkers are more prone to simplifying problems in order to reduce uncertainty and information overload. As a result, they may realize after the fact that they failed to recognize important information.

Thinking as a Team

The recognition (or creation) of opportunity is a critical stage of entrepreneurship, one that the concept of entrepreneurial alertness addresses directly. But complex, creative, or integrative thinking is needed throughout the establishment and development of a business. Entrepreneurs and other business leaders have to implement their ideas in rapidly changing, usually highly competitive contexts and they must formulate and implement effective strategy for the maintenance and growth of the enterprise. For this, the cognitive framing or mental models that drive strategic decision making are as important as those that make it possible to recognize opportunity. They direct attention to new information and emerging trends, evoke lessons derived from similar past events and conditions, frame interpretations of problems and opportunities, and serve as the basis for predictions about alternative courses of action and also therefore for judgments about how best to allocate resources (West, 2007).

These are deeply intellectual capacities reflecting explicit and implicit knowledge from a wide range of fields, not mechanistic or technical skills. If they appear to be intuitive rather than intellectually grounded, that is only because expertise eventually becomes automatic, giving the impression of being intuitive when, in fact, it emerges from deep experience and understanding. This cognitive conception of the foundations of effective entrepreneurship and business leadership offers a very different perspective on how to educate for innovation and entrepreneurship than the widely held perception that "successful entrepreneurs are born, not made," a view we heard from virtually all the business people and many of the educators we consulted.

The fact that entrepreneurial founders and leaders are almost always teams rather than single individuals adds an additional layer of complexity to the way that evolving, though often implicit, mental models guide strategic decision making. Founding or senior management teams need to forge shared frames of interpretation from their initial diversity of perspective. This means that success requires not only fresh and insightful thinking—or in Martin's terms, integrative thinking—but also the co-creation of visions, interpretations, and judgments. The team must forge a *shared* understanding of what it is after, what the central threats and opportunities are, and how to resolve inevitable tensions between maintaining the focus and momentum of the initial direction and adapting to changing circumstances.

West (2007) refers to this shared sense-making as "collective cognition." Idea and knowledge diversity in the team contributes to its ability to acquire and make good use of resources but may make it more difficult to achieve a cohesive point of view. Doing so requires team leaders and members to understand the different perceptions, starting assumptions, and interpretations that each person brings; to take the best ideas from different perspectives into account in creating a shared working model to guide decision making; and to move from multiple points of view to a unified collective cognition that is stronger than any one member's initial perspective. None of this is easy and the process succeeds only if group members are skilled in recognizing the kernels of good ideas expressed by others and building productively on them. This requires careful listening, open-mindedness, good judgment, and intellectual creativity—capacities that students can develop in well-run humanities seminars, in the best of the team projects that are so prevalent in undergraduate business education, and even in late night conversations about what advocates of liberal education call "the big questions."

Innovation as a Team-Based Process

West's (2007) research on team-based innovation is consistent with the approaches of some highly visible companies in Silicon Valley, where The Carnegie Foundation for the Advancement of Teaching is located. In his book, *The Ten Faces of Innovation* (Kelley & Littman, 2005), Tom Kelley, cofounder of the highly acclaimed design firm IDEO that is headquartered in Palo Alto, describes innovation in terms that are reminiscent of Gaglio and Katz's description of entrepreneurial alertness and Roger Martin's conception of integrative thinking. (It is worth noting that IDEO CEO, Tim Brown, is one of Martin's exemplary business leaders and *The Opposable Mind* uses IDEO's work to illustrate the value of integrative thinking.) According to Kelley, the process of innovative design involves open-mindedness and intellectual humility, agility, and flexibility, as well as a tendency to question one's own worldview and "be open to new insights every day" (p. 19). Kelley describes freshness and creativity of thinking by quoting Albert von Szent-Györgyi's belief that discovery "consists of seeing what everyone else has seen and thinking what no one else has thought" (p. 19). Creative thinking comes in part from curiosity and an exploratory mind-set—that is, from some (at least implicit) recognition that one's customary intellectual frame is only one among many, an orientation that frees thinking from conventional categories and assumptions.

Kelley conceives the process of design or innovation as a group rather than individual endeavor and describes a number of valuable roles that group members play when innovative design work goes well. The "anthropologist," for example, "brings new learning and insights into the organization by observing human behavior and developing a deep understanding of how people interact physically and emotionally with products, services, and spaces" (p. 9). Successful anthropologists (who are not necessarily trained in that field) bring fresh eyes to their observations of people, clearing away preconceptions and relying on a kind of empathic understanding and close attention to nuance. But, even without their conscious awareness, the intuitions of the most insightful and creative observers are grounded in rich knowledge and experience and in conceptual schemes through which they interpret and organize what they are seeing.

Based on their insights about potential users of the product or service, Kelley explains, team members playing the anthropologist role are often able to reframe the central task or problem in ways that spark a breakthrough solution. One team working for a soft drink company in Poland was looking for ways to increase sales at train stations, for example. As they observed a busy train station in Warsaw, they noticed that travelers often glanced nervously at the soft drink displays, then at their watches, then back at the display. It seemed that these passengers wanted to buy a drink for the journey but were worried about missing the train. When the anthropologists set up a kiosk selling soft drinks that also included a large clock, sales shot up.

Another important group member is the "cross-pollinator," whose job is to explore other cultures, domains, and industries and bring insights from those explorations back to the home enterprise. The cross-pollinator role involves "creating something new through the unexpected juxtaposition of seemingly unrelated ideas" (p. 68). Among other things, cross-pollinators know how to think in metaphors, which allows them to see how insights from one field can be relevant for a very different field. In this way, they are able to see connections and patterns that others miss.

These and other "faces of innovation" that Kelley and his IDEO colleagues have drawn from years of innovative design experience underline our argument that business innovation is nurtured by liberal learning: a rich and diverse knowledge base, reflective habits of mind, and an explorer mentality characterized by intellectual playfulness and agility. This is the same point that Gaglio and Katz make when they suggest that strong linkages among rich, well-developed schemas enable alert individuals to see opportunities that are invisible to others. That, along with effective implementation, is the essence of innovation.

In work that builds on his earlier articulation of integrative thinking, Roger Martin's 2009 book, *The Design of Business*, explicates the critical role of design thinking in business success and organizational value creation more generally. "The most successful businesses in the years to come," he argues, "will balance analytical mastery and intuitive originality in a dynamic interplay," identified as "design thinking" (p. 6). *The Design of Business* acknowledges the essential part played by Analytical Thinking in the task of continually redesigning a business but points also to the limitations of this mode of thinking, suggesting that creative insight is also essential. In our terms, this points to the need for business education to go beyond training in technical skills and analysis to include Multiple Framing and the Reflective Exploration of Meaning.

Social Impact

There is no question that innovation is as essential to a flourishing economy as it is to our capacity as human beings to address the big challenges we face. But, although it is clear that technological and social innovations have dramatic effects on the quality of life for people everywhere, these effects are not always beneficial. The impacts of innovation are sometimes good, sometimes bad, and often mixed or indeterminate. Tim Brown, CEO and cofounder of IDEO, wrote in his book, *Change by Design* (2009) that a purely technocratic view of innovation is less sustainable now than ever. The world needs new products and approaches that balance the interests of individuals and society as a whole. It needs new strategies that result in differences that matter and a sense of purpose that engages everyone affected by those strategies. It needs a human-centered rather technology-centered worldview guiding innovation.

We have argued throughout this book that undergraduate business education needs to be informed by and directed toward the fundamental social purpose of business, the creation of inclusive and sustainable prosperity. Similarly, if innovation is to help solve rather than exacerbate the world's pressing problems, innovators have to think about and take some responsibility for the likely impact of their creations.

The field of engineering has begun to take this challenge seriously and engineering education may therefore provide clues for business educators about how to prepare students to think about and be responsible for the outcomes of their work. In our study of engineering education, we found that some core values, including public safety and environmental sustainability, are threaded throughout the curriculum—in engineering science and laboratory courses as well as in courses on design. At many universities, engineering design courses include modules on ethics and social impact, and students are asked to speak to the likely environmental and human effects of the products they are designing. As we noted in our book on engineering education, a student in one such course told us, "An engineer is someone who uses math and science to mess with the world—by designing and making things that people will buy and use; and once you mess with the world, you are responsible for the mess you've made" (Sheppard, Macatangay, Sullivan, & Colby, 2009, p. ix).

Formation of Entrepreneurial Character

We have stressed in this book and elsewhere that a full undergraduate education must convey knowledge and skill and also form character (Colby, Ehrlich, Beaumont, & Stephens, 2003). Clearly this is true in education for innovation and entrepreneurship. Cognitive skills and expertise are essential to such work, but managing high-risk endeavors so that they flourish in the long term also requires persistence, stamina, diligence, commitment, realistic optimism, and a sense of direction or purpose. In fact, even developing the cognitive dimensions—the fine-tuned thinking and creativity that are needed for success—requires these personal qualities. The process of character formation around such traits represents another important link between liberal learning and preparation for entrepreneurship, including both business and social entrepreneurship.

Research on the sources of extraordinary persistence, determination, and commitment suggests why liberal learning is so well suited to formation for successful entrepreneurship. This research points to three qualities shared by successful entrepreneurs and creative people in many fields:

a strong sense of purpose, intrinsic motivation or love of the activity itself, and a drive for excellence. Both Tom Kelley's and Roger Martin's reflections on the process of successful innovation include the observation that many important innovations—such as the Linux operating system, for example—are driven by purpose and passion as essential motivators. This observation is consistent with research on creativity and innovation. Case studies of exceptionally creative people suggest that creative people share a deep sense of purpose and strong emotional ties to their endeavors (Gruber, 1981).

In *The Opposable Mind*, Martin refers to this sense of purpose as an aspect of "stance"—that is, how you see the world around you and how you see yourself in that world. Integrative thinkers are constantly driven to improve their understanding of the contexts and issues their companies confront, continually developing more subtle and accurate conceptions of those issues. They are not content with competence, always striving, instead, to increase their own expertise and the excellence of their organizations. Their motivation is rooted in their stance, their understanding of the world, and their place in it.

Psychological studies that have explored the development of ever-deepening expertise support Martin's interpretation. Most notably, Bereiter and Scardamalia (1993) have shown that it takes curiosity and intrinsic fascination with the work along with deep commitment to its purposes to propel people toward ever-greater excellence. One of the less-than-encouraging findings of Bereiter and Scardamalia's work is that most people fail to become true experts in this sense, allowing themselves to plateau at routine levels of competence.

These and other studies of people who strive constantly for something better underscore the powerful roles played by sense of purpose, social contribution, and Martin's notion of stance. In our terms, this points to the importance of the Reflective Exploration of Meaning in establishing a powerfully motivating sense of direction, which contributes in turn to entrepreneurial success and other kinds of achievement through the character traits it engenders, such as persistence and resilience in the face of challenge.

Independent strands of research by Teresa Amabile and Mihaly Csikszentmihalyi converge on the importance of a related issue: the importance of intrinsic motivation. As Howard Gardner points out in his comprehensive analysis of this and other research on creativity, creative solutions to problems are more likely to occur when people engage in an activity for the sheer enjoyment of it than when they are driven by external rewards (Gardner, 1993). Amabile's case studies of highly creative people, for example, reveal that these people "tend from their earliest days to be explorers, innovators, tinkerers, experimenting all the time, even at earliest stages of learning the field" (Gardner, 1993, p. 32). Tom Kelley also stresses the intrinsically rewarding quality of many of the activities involved in innovation. For example, the team members that Kelley calls the "organizing personas"—those who have mastered the processes by which organizations move ideas forward—do not dismiss an administrative task such as budgeting as red tape. Instead, "they recognize it as a complex game of chess, and they play to win" (Kelley & Littman, 2005, p. 9).

Another quality of successful entrepreneurs is what David McClelland (1976) called *achievement motivation*. McClelland distinguished achievement motivation, which involves a drive for the intrinsic rewards of excellence, from the desire for extrinsic rewards such as money or power over others. Research evidence is strong that business owners have a higher need for achievement than other populations and that entrepreneurs' need for achievement is positively correlated with the success of their businesses (Collins, Hanges, & Locke, 2004; Rauch & Frese, 2007). Individuals high in achievement motivation see financial rewards more as indicators of competence than as ends in themselves.

Educational Implications

All of these personal characteristics point to the values and outcomes associated with high-quality liberal learning: an intrinsic fascination with ideas and with learning itself; a desire to achieve excellence for its own sake; an exploratory orientation toward complex and challenging ideas, systems, and tasks; and a strong sense of social and personal direction or purpose. Of course, these qualities can be present in professional studies as well but education that is narrowly instrumental or driven largely by anticipated extrinsic rewards, such as salary, is likely to undermine the very qualities that foster innovation.

As we have outlined here, contemporary research on the psychology of entrepreneurship also draws attention to the importance of cognitive dimensions such as highly organized yet constantly evolving mental models. It has been clear for some time that successful entrepreneurs are characterized less by high risk tolerance than by capacities that help them creatively limit and manage risk. Some of these capacities are the kinds of intuitive street smarts that typify experts in every domain—knowledge and understanding so finely attuned, so deeply grasped, that they become automatic and seemingly intuitive. We have also outlined an approach to innovation that is very much oriented to the value of insight and the quality of thought and imagination. We offer this picture of the cognitive and personal factors supporting innovation and successful entrepreneurship as a guide to education for innovation and entrepreneurial success. And we believe that this way of thinking about educational goals and outcomes could be used to facilitate a much wider infusion of these concerns into undergraduate business education—and indeed throughout undergraduate education, whatever the major.

It seems clear from the research literature on successful entrepreneurship and innovation that teaching the basic business disciplines is necessary but not sufficient. Similarly, courses in which students develop business plans can foster innovative thinking and deepen students' understanding of the broad contexts of business, but, taken alone, these courses do not ensure strong preparation for innovative, entrepreneurial corporate leaders or founders of new businesses or social ventures.

Instead, coursework needs to stimulate fascination with a wide array of subject matters and phenomena, including many that have no immediately obvious implications for business success. It should also provide repeated experience playing with ideas, seeing connections and parallels across diverse domains, seeking to understand unexpected events and make sense of anomalies, integrating seemingly disparate ideas, and revising existing conceptions and assumptions as needed to gain a better grasp on experience. This kind of planned, structured practice with innovative, integrative, entrepreneurial thinking helps build an enduring capacity to approach complexity in a productive way (Martin, 2007). Successful entrepreneurs need a broad, rich knowledge base, the ability to see patterns, an explorer mentality, intellectual flexibility, and a willingness to question basic assumptions—all characteristics of a liberally educated person.

Although our site visits did not provide many well-elaborated examples of this approach to teaching for entrepreneurial, creative, or integrative thinking and orientation, some courses and programs are clearly moving in this direction. For example, recognition of the important roles played by the appreciation of complexity and a strong sense of purpose was reflected in several of the entrepreneurship courses we observed. In NYU's Entrepreneurship and the Law, Professor Richard Hendler helps students understand the legal, policy, and organizational contexts of entrepreneurship and, in the process, addresses the social impact of business and its relationship with an enduring sense of purpose. During our class visit, Hendler asked students to think about questions such as "What's the public good of investment banking?" and his syllabus ends with the bolded exhortation to **"Remember to search for and find passion in your life!"**

Standard courses on the development of business plans also have the potential to promote innovative thinking, sensitivity to assumptions, and a deeper grasp of the social-historical contexts of entrepreneurship; some of those we visited appear to do this. For example, Babson's Entrepreneurship and New Ventures requires students to situate their ideas in the context of social trends that bear on their ventures, consider the relevance of broader questions such as intellectual property law, and pay attention to ethical concerns such as fairness within the management team.

Bentley University offers a program called Complex Problems, Creative Solutions (CPCS) that represents an interesting approach to teaching for innovative problem solving—one that makes the program useful preparation for both social and business entrepreneurship. Under the direction of the associate dean of arts and sciences, an economic geographer, the program engages participating students in two years of coursework organized around an overarching theme. The theme we observed was called "The Unintended Consequences of Consumer Choices," with particular attention to environmental sustainability and technology, along with "technology trash." Courses are organized to provide a coherent experience in understanding and developing responses to this complex problem; they meet both business and general education core requirements. Students put together individualized courses of study within the program, all of which draw from a range of business and arts and sciences disciplines.

Courses designated as parts of the CPCS curriculum represent efforts to teach for many of the outcomes that research on innovative thinking points to as important, such as rich contextual understanding. American Environmental History, for example, examines the interactions between human societies and the natural world, tracing environmental history in the United States from early Native American practices to the present day. Students examine environmental history in terms of the intersection of landscapes, ideologies, and technologies and the course aims to help them make connections between disparate events and time periods.

Environmental Chemistry, which fulfills the institution's general education science requirement, also fits into the Complex Problems program, exploring the basic principles of chemistry as they relate to questions of pollution and environmental protection. Other courses—The Legal and Ethical Environment of Business, Problems in Philosophy, Human Behavior and Organizations, and Advanced Inquiry in Writing—

contribute a wide range of perspectives on the problem under consideration and creative approaches to its solution. Course experiences are supplemented by cocurricular opportunities that include guest lectures, film screenings, community events, and service-learning projects.

The Bentley CPCS initiative is notable for its focus on social innovation as well as the more general qualities of complexity and creative problem solving. This focus may enhance its capacity to support the formation of important personal qualities we described previously in this chapter. Likewise, some of the efforts currently being developed to teach for social entrepreneurship may be especially relevant for supporting a strong sense of purpose and the other personal qualities that are known to contribute to entrepreneurial success.

A handful of national initiatives to support ambitious approaches to social entrepreneurship education are now spawning programs at U.S. colleges and universities. Among the most developed are those coming out of the Transformative Action Institute (TAI), founded by Scott Sherman. TAI helps campuses develop multidisciplinary courses in social entrepreneurship or social innovation. These courses have been taught at Princeton, Yale, UCLA, UC Berkeley, NYU, Johns Hopkins, and other universities. Among their strengths is attention to helping students shape a sense of purpose for themselves, think through ethical issues such as consistency between ethical means and ends, and understand the history and complexity of previous efforts to promote social change.

In this chapter, we have focused on a handful of issues that we believe should be urgent learning priorities in the preparation of organizational and business leaders for the demands our troubled world faces right now: the capacities to function effectively in a globally connected world, to generate creative solutions to complicated problems, to develop innovations that contribute to human welfare, and to mobilize resources toward the creation of both economic and broader human value.

Despite the timeliness of these issues and the urgency associated with them, these themes also reflect longer-term imperatives. It is hard to imagine a world that does not need innovative problem solving, creative design, and effective deployment of resources to take full advantage of opportunities. Likewise, it will always be important to grapple with pluralism and the important interactions among different social institutions across time and place.

All of these themes reveal the limits of a narrowly instrumental perspective that does not build on and contribute to a wider angle of vision. All require students to draw on expanded knowledge and experience well beyond the business disciplines, at least as they are conventionally taught.

We believe that these important learning outcomes should be woven through the undergraduate business curriculum. And we are convinced that in order to achieve these goals, business students must have a liberal education that enables them to make sense of the world and their place in it. In the culminating chapter of this book, we set forth our recommendations for pushing this vision ahead.

9

THE WAY FORWARD

THE WHARTON SCHOOL at the University of Pennsylvania is ranked at the very top among undergraduate business programs by *U.S. News & World Report* (2010). Reviewing its history, we are struck by the fact that a half-century ago, in the late 1950s and 1960s, there was more structural integration of liberal arts and business at Wharton than is true today. The departments of economics, sociology, political science, and regional science were all part of Wharton in that era, which is no longer true. As described in an intellectual history of the school, there were strong, collaborative ties between faculty in the social sciences and faculty who taught the core required business courses, and this led to a "close and vibrant connection between economic theory and practical policy" (Sass, 1982, p. 287).

What makes this account even more striking is that, even then, in the midst of what appears to be an impressive level of integration, there was a sense that it was not enough. In 1958, a board of consultants commissioned by the Wharton School found that undergraduates were lacking in liberal arts education and in the integration of their liberal learning with their business education. The location of the social science departments within Wharton was a strength of the school, the authors reported, but this strength had not been fully realized (The Board of Consultants, 1958).

Rather, they concluded, "the traditional Wharton claim to providing a broad liberal education along with business training is not at present being achieved. Nor is the oft-cited claim to an integrated program made possible by virtue of the four-year program which takes the student into both business and non-business subjects in each year being realized."

Students were found to be "taking more specialized business training, less work in the humanities, and negligible work in the sciences, foreign languages, and mathematics" (pp. 25–26). To remedy the problem, the board of consultants proposed a radical revision of the curriculum that would include courses during the first three years in what they called integrated behavioral science, integrated science, integrated humanities, and integrated social science, along with comprehensive quantitative and comprehensive communications sequences. Only after this "rigorous" curriculum, as the report described it, would students be able to take courses in business fields such as accounting, marketing, finance, and management, and they would need to attend Wharton for a fifth year to receive both an undergraduate degree and a masters degree in either business administration or governmental administration.

Readers will not, perhaps, be surprised that these recommendations were not adopted. Instead, in the 1970s, the social sciences moved out of Wharton and into a newly created faculty of arts and sciences. The reasons had apparently little to do with curricular judgments about what made sense for undergraduates but were rooted, rather, in the desire of the faculty and a new university president to unite the arts and sciences. As chronicled in the Wharton history, "The institutional consensus concluded that the social sciences were now sufficiently liberal for admission into the heart of scholarship; it determined that it was in the best interest of the university, if not of the Wharton School, to unite the various social science departments with those of the liberal arts and sciences" (Sass, 1982, p. 288).

This story seems worth retelling as background to our recommendations for today's business education programs because the tale makes clear that proposals for integration are not new—they surface repeatedly in the field's history of reforms—but neither is strong resistance. Change is hard. It requires a strong vision of possible alternatives, courage and persistence, resources, and a compelling perception of need that is widely understood and embraced by business leaders, faculty, administrators, and, ultimately, students.

The Need for Reform, Revisited

We stressed at the outset of this book that the question, "What should an undergraduate business education provide for students?" can be answered only by addressing the more basic issue, "What should a *college* education provide?" In responding to that more fundamental query, we argued that college is a time for students to expand and deepen their sense of who they are and how they relate to the world around them. The undergraduate experience is a time of transition when students should not only acquire the knowledge and skills they need to make their way after graduation, but also expand their intellectual horizons, come to appreciate perspectives that differ from their own, and ultimately gain a sense of the kinds of contributions they want to make to the world.

Since its earliest days, U.S. higher education has sought to provide the knowledge, the skills, and especially the dispositions for graduates to become active and constructive civic leaders. Much of our prior work at the Carnegie Foundation has been focused on ways that colleges and universities can promote undergraduate civic education, and business majors certainly need that education. Survey data show, in fact, that the more credit hours in business taken by undergraduates, the less likely they are to be committed to civic participation (Nie & Hillygus, 2001).

Along with preparation for responsible citizenship in a general sense, business students need to develop as civic leaders *within* the business domain. For this, they need a sophisticated understanding of the effects business has on society and also of the implications that other social institutions hold for business. This orientation toward social purpose and significance is the mind-set that marks professional fields such as law and medicine, one that is much needed for our national well-being as well as for individuals' vocational and personal fulfillment. A strong liberal education, well integrated with preparation in business, has the potential to foster precisely this kind of professional orientation.

If business majors are to achieve these goals, the liberal learning dimensions of their education need to be taken seriously, addressed systematically, and fully integrated with their career preparation. Indeed, although our study focused on business education, we believe it is no less important that majors in other disciplines, including not only vocational fields such as engineering and nursing but also the arts and sciences, gain a strong liberal education that enables them to understand the world and their place in it and that prepares them to contribute to the life of their times.

Regrettably, many undergraduate business programs do not provide strong liberal learning integrated with preparation for careers in business. This means that their students miss the chance to develop the skills, knowledge, and dispositions they need to be effective in business as well as in life. Their education is too narrow to support the creativity and flexibility they will need to be innovative business leaders. In many cases it also fails to prepare them as fully as it could for their roles as citizens and as thoughtful, intellectually vibrant individuals.

For business students, who tend to focus very intently on career preparation, general education courses are especially likely to be seen as marginal to the real purposes of their education. This means that, for them, the curricular barbell of general education and the major is often heavily tilted toward the business education end. The tilt may be accentuated by the fact that core subjects in business, such as accounting and finance, emphasize various forms of analysis, which, although demanding, present students with problems that have clear, right-or-wrong answers. By contrast, in many courses in the arts and sciences disciplines, particularly the humanities, students encounter and must manage significant ambiguity and uncertainty. In our site visits, we often heard from students and from faculty commenting about students that those in the arts and sciences enjoy engaging with big questions that cannot yield simple, clear-cut answers, and business students, similar to their peers in engineering, feel less comfortable with ambiguity and subjectivity. Courses that focus on open-ended questions that involve significant interpretation and reflection are, therefore, not likely to be favorites with many business students. This circumstance effectively tilts the balance even further toward business and away from the liberal arts.

The narrowness that results is then intensified by the fact that business courses often rely on a few influential conceptual models that are repeated throughout the curriculum and seldom subjected to searching reflection and questioning. The continual use of models in a taken-for-granted way can lead students to experience them as literal representations of the world rather than as conceptual tools that are grounded in particular theoretical frameworks through which to simplify and operate on phenomena that are more complex than the model is able to represent. Students rarely confront the assumptions on which these models rest or consider fundamentally different ways to frame the phenomena in question.

More specifically, in many core business courses, students regularly are presented with a model of business activity drawn primarily from neoclassical economics. This model, sometimes summed up as the *efficient market hypothesis*, presents a highly idealized conception of market behavior in which many individual firms' pursuit of competitive advantage is assumed—rather than empirically demonstrated—to result in optimal states of efficiency in the employment of human and material resources. When this simplified conceptual picture is presented as the actual context of business activity, the models of business enterprise must also be represented as analytically complex but essentially one-dimensional strategies of competition. When classroom practices involving these models employ individual or team competitions, they reinforce the theoretical emphasis.

Without countervailing viewpoints, students can come to believe that such a relentless, often zero-sum, competitive process is not merely a hypothetical model but a description of all that is important in business. Although, when asked, most faculty endorse a multifaceted stakeholder value approach (rather than an approach oriented solely to shareholder value), this more inclusive perspective on business enterprise is far from pervasive in the day-to-day classroom teaching of the core disciplines. All of this seriously narrows business students' understanding of business and its relation to the larger world.

Courses in the liberal arts and sciences are a potential antidote to this narrow view, certainly. But, in the absence of special efforts toward integration, the business majors we spoke to rarely make connections between their experience in those settings and what they learn in the business curriculum. Structured opportunities to see how insights from arts and sciences disciplines can provide wisdom about the things that concern them most urgently are few and far between. And if liberal learning is not intentionally connected with students' central concerns, it may be decorative or entertaining but will not be deeply formative.

What *is* deeply formative is the totality of the undergraduate business student experience. The curriculum is a major contributor to that totality but it is far from the only one. The cocurriculum and the campus culture reinforce curricular messages. Popular cocurricular activities for business students often include clubs and organizations—such as those in accounting or finance—that allow them to start pursuing their intended careers as quickly as possible, along with case competitions, business-plan competitions, investment competitions, and many games and simulations with a competitive thrust. In this sense, the cocurriculum experienced by business students may intensify the focus on preparation for careers and reinforce the orientation toward competition as a defining feature of institutional and individual relationships.

A spirit of competition also pervades business schools' relationships with each other. This competition is crystallized in significant part by attention to school rankings, especially those of *U.S. News & World Report* and *Business Week*. These rankings are based in factors such as reputation and the job placement of graduates and do not give credit for efforts to integrate liberal learning with preparation for business. Thus, they too intensify the institution's focus on career preparation, narrowly defined, and on competition as a defining feature of business.

Other aspects of the campus culture in many business schools reflect this focus and energy around the competitive pursuit of career advancement. The presence of corporate recruiters as well as the constant buzz about how recent graduates are faring on the job market are vivid reminders of the central goal of the college experience. Along the way, students are intent on securing summer internships and pursuing other means to bolster and polish their credentials. Although faculty and administrative leaders explain the value of double majors that pair business with a liberal arts discipline, students see greater value in dual business majors or several business minors or concentrations. Meanwhile, more luxurious facilities, higher paid faculty, and exclusive access to certain resources underscore the separation of the business department or school from the rest of the university.

This sense of separation from the larger undergraduate experience is underlined as well in the fact that the curricula of undergraduate business and the MBA are similar in subject matter and that MBA students sometimes act as teaching assistants or mentors in undergraduate business courses. This can be a very beneficial experience for both groups of students. But shared experiences and facilities, along with joint administrative oversight, can pull undergraduate business students even more fully into the business school orbit and away from a collegiate experience that is fully shared with their classmates in the arts and sciences.

Five Recommendations

Against this summary of challenges, we offer five recommendations for strengthening undergraduate business education. Most of them could apply equally to other undergraduate professional fields but business education is well positioned to lead the way. Because it is the biggest undergraduate major, because the field is rich with human and institutional resources, and because it prepares students for positions of exceptional power and impact, new directions in business education are likely to be high in both visibility and status. Thus, the immediate beneficiaries of new directions would be business school students and faculty, but there is great potential for positive impact beyond that immediate scope.

Recommendation One: A strong liberal education should be part of the undergraduate experience for every business major.

The central aim of a college education, whatever the major or special concentration, should be to shape the minds and character of students so that they can make sense of the world and their place in it and responsibly engage with the life of their times. Toward these ends, liberal education requires academic content knowledge and several dimensions of cognitive skills as well as the capacity to bring knowledge and skills to bear on complex and ambiguous real-world issues.

Clearly, if students are to make sense of the world, they need insights from a wide array of arts and science disciplines as well as from business. Simply taking courses from a variety of fields is not sufficient, however. The material must be taught with integration in mind, coming together in ways that students can draw on in their personal and civic lives as well as in their work. It should also be taught in ways most likely to stimulate a fascination with ideas and an exploratory mind-set.

We have argued throughout this book that a high-quality liberal education must include, along with engagement across multiple domains of knowledge, three essential modes of thinking. Analytical Thinking, a central goal of both arts and sciences and business disciplines—the coin of the academic realm, one might say—entails the translation of concrete experience into general concepts and categories and logical thinking using those concepts and categories. Multiple Framing represents that aspect of liberal learning that recognizes competing, even conflicting, perspectives for viewing the world. And the Reflective Exploration of Meaning engages learners with questions of purpose, commitment, and value. Educators in all disciplines need to pay explicit attention to these intellectual capacities if students are to attain them. At the present time, Analytical Thinking receives the greatest attention in both business and liberal arts and sciences; curricula in both arenas would be strengthened by paying more attention to Multiple Framing and the Reflective Exploration of Meaning.

Additionally, higher education must prepare its students to *use* their knowledge and intellectual capacities to act effectively and responsibly in the world. Too often educators assume that if students gain disciplinary content knowledge and analytical capacities, they will automatically be able to bring their learning productively to bear when they need to make decisions and judgments in complex circumstances of practice. But generalized conceptual knowledge is not sufficient to guide judgments about particular, unique situations. This is why we include Practical Reasoning as another essential aim of liberal learning. Practical Reasoning is the ability to navigate the necessary back-and-forth between general concepts and particular challenges and responsibilities, making it possible to take advantage of knowledge and intellectual capacities to think flexibly; see and evaluate a range of options; form good judgments based in knowledge, understanding, rigorous analysis, and integrity; and manage the unfolding implementation of their decisions and plans, often in contexts of considerable uncertainty and constantly changing dynamics.

Recommendation Two: Liberal learning should be incorporated into the undergraduate business curriculum.

Students need to learn to think broadly and creatively about complex issues, develop sophisticated modes of thinking, and explore questions of personal meaning in their business courses as well as in the arts and sciences so that their college experience will form a more coherent whole. And the incorporation of liberal learning into the business curriculum can make it more likely that students will see the relevance of that learning for their work and be able to draw on it productively as their careers develop. Studies of successful business leaders have shown that their thinking patterns involve not only Analytical Thinking but also something more like Multiple Framing and a sense of purpose developed through processes that we call the Reflective Exploration of Meaning. These leaders fully appreciate that there are several fundamentally different ways of making sense of complex phenomena and they find ways to create a synthesis that incorporates the strengths of varied conceptual frames.

Incorporating the spirit of liberal learning into business departments can also help change the tone of students' approach to their education. We have reported that, at least in the eyes of students, study in the arts and sciences is said to have a quality in which the discovery and exploration of ideas carries an intrinsic fascination in addition to whatever practical value it may also provide. For business students, the focus is more sharply instrumental: teach me what I need to know and be able to do to succeed in my career. As different as these two attitudes may seem, we have seen that effective programs can bring them together to the great benefit of many student outcomes.

Studies of innovative design and creativity more generally have shown that an exploratory, playful, intrinsically fascinated orientation underlies the creative process in any domain. Given this understanding of what is needed for creative thinking in business, it makes sense to try to give business students a more exploratory and intellectually vibrant stance toward their studies and their work. This means bringing liberal learning ways of thinking about the world more fully and visibly into the courses and experiences students participate in as business majors.

*Recommendation Three: Business and arts and sciences
curricula should be linked together in ways that help
students make connections.*

We use the metaphor of a double helix to represent the possibility of
ongoing, structured curricular integration. We first encountered the
double helix metaphor when faculty and administrators at Santa Clara
University explained to us their goals for the core undergraduate curriculum they were fashioning at the time—clusters of carefully designed and
linked courses to integrate learning in general education and the majors,
including business and other vocational majors—through a focus on
themes that cut across traditional disciplines.

Of course some students may discover for themselves connections
across their various courses and experience—whether out of an integrative impulse or purely by happenstance. But this is not good enough.
Campuses that put in place purposeful structures for integration—be it
through linked or clustered courses, special integrative projects, capstone
experiences, portfolios, or some other approach—greatly raise the chances
that *all* students will have the double helix experience. The integration
of liberal learning and business is too important to be left to chance.

We encountered a number of ways to accomplish this. Some programs
are themselves located at the intersection of arts and sciences and business education. Others create either required or optional tracks within
the business curriculum that directly link liberal learning and business.
Still other programs create integrative, thematically focused clusters of
newly created or already existing courses. Within and beyond these curricular structures, programs pursuing an integrative approach bring a
breadth of content, perspective, and innovative pedagogy to many
required and elective courses. All of these approaches can be effective if
they are designed with the integration of business and liberal learning as
a central goal.

Recommendation Four: Institutions should be intentional *in their
integration of the arts and sciences and business education.*

Ambitiously integrative programs of the kind we have described require
institutional commitment, leadership, and continued monitoring and
development over time. In these programs, administrative leaders and
faculty collaborate to shape a set of mutually reinforcing experiences for
students that provide an educational whole that is more than its separate
parts. This requires institutional intentionality.

Institutional intentionality is a deceptively simple concept that is remarkably difficult to achieve in higher education. It is the key to learning that lasts in the integration of the arts and sciences and business education, just as it is to systematic advances in other higher education reform agendas (Colby et al., 2003; Colby, Beaumont, Ehrlich, & Corngold, 2007). An institutionwide perspective helps to ensure multiple, reinforcing interventions that are designed with a clear set of learning objectives in mind and implemented through educational programs that are well aligned with those objectives (Wiggins & McTighe, 2005).

In this spirit, it is important to remember that the curriculum does not represent the whole of the undergraduate experience. When the integration of liberal and business learning includes not only the curriculum but also the cocurriculum and the campus climate—all inter-related and mutually reinforcing—the impact can be even more substantial. Institutions should aim to create a powerful and coherent culture that draws students from all departments together around inspiring themes and underlines the many ways of contributing to the greater good.

Finally, institutional intentionality requires educational leaders to know the extent to which integrative objectives are actually being addressed and achieved: systematically gathering, analyzing, and acting on evidence about what is and is not working. The current national emphasis on assessment for accountability has powerful outside champions, as readers well know, but the importance of assessment data and deliberation is also an internal imperative, key (as students learn in many a business course) to the process of ongoing improvement. Programs seeking to integrate liberal learning with business education must bring this objective to their assessment and program evaluation efforts.

Recommendation Five: Business educators have a great deal to contribute to teaching and learning in the arts and sciences.

Especially if business programs are able to overcome the false dichotomy between an intellectually exciting education and a practically useful one, they can help the arts and sciences move toward the same ideal: a college education that is an intellectually exciting preparation for a life that aspires to worldly achievement along with an enduring sense of fascination and love of learning.

Business education is particularly strong on the practical side of this equation and is able to share highly developed pedagogical strategies for teaching Practical Reasoning and for making abstract concepts real through simulations and other forms of active learning. Business education is also notably strong in the degree to which it takes seriously and effectively pursues preparation for life in a globally interconnected world.

We have said that business students must understand the business sector as one social institution among many and must come to appreciate the responsibility entailed in gaining influence within such a powerful force for affecting human welfare. Likewise, undergraduates in other majors could benefit greatly by understanding better the nature of business and its important role in society. All students today live in a world that is shaped and directed to a large degree by the business sector; most have frighteningly little sense of what that means. We therefore recommend that colleges and universities consider including courses for all undergraduates that help them understand business, its modes of organizing and operating, and its roles and responsibilities in society. We do not suggest a single path for implementing this recommendation. Some institutions offer courses on business within the arts and sciences but there are certainly many other ways to achieve this goal.

The Way Forward: An Action Agenda

These recommendations are broad ones. Embracing and working toward them is a significant commitment and a long-term process. Diverse perspectives must be brought to bear. Local circumstances and culture can play catalyzing but also confounding roles in the process. Difficult dialogues will probably be necessary. And there must be leadership—at all levels. Concretely, then, what are the most productive ways to begin and what tasks and topics will help build consensus and momentum? In this final section, we propose six action items that we believe can help campuses move toward the integrative vision laid out in this book. They are not meant as sequential steps, though the first is in a sense an all-encompassing item intended to create a context for the others.

Bring the community of stakeholders together to take stock.

This book features inspiring examples from programs and campuses that are committed to bringing liberal learning and business education together in ways that make a difference for students. But those programs did not, of course, materialize out of thin air. The kinds of changes we are advocating are best begun in conversation, when gathering evidence, and when engaging in critical reflection about who has a stake in undergraduate business education. Thus, a first step is to assemble appropriate stakeholders and establish a process for taking stock of the current program's capacity to prepare business undergraduates for work and for life.

This process can begin on a small scale with faculty and administrators within the business program but, as discussion evolves, others should be invited to the table, including selected faculty from arts and sciences disciplines, leaders from the local business community (or perhaps members of an outside advisory board), and students.

What is the best way to stimulate constructive conversation? We recommend putting evidence into the picture as early as possible and much of the best, most relevant evidence already exists: course syllabi, case studies, student projects or papers, final exams (questions and also student responses if possible), and other products of the work that faculty and students already do in the regular routines of teaching and learning. Seen in the different context of a broad review (rather than as discrete classroom products), artifacts such as these can reveal a great deal about de facto goals, methods, and outcomes of the program, opening the way for discussion about whether, how, and how well integrative aims are reflected. Additionally, the group may decide that further information and perspectives are needed, in which case simple surveys can be designed and administered, whether to capture more about student perspectives or to canvas faculty opinion more widely. Our own experience on campus visits points to the power of one-on-one interviews and focus groups as well.

What questions should guide the gathering and analysis of evidence? There is no quick answer to this question, but readers will not be surprised that we suggest this book as a source of questions. Do the accounts of business education we have put forward resonate with local realities? Where does the program stand in terms of its capacity to provide business students with a robust liberal education? Where are the strengths? Weaknesses? Special circumstances? Other questions might include the following:

- How is our undergraduate business program different from the MBA? Is the undergraduate program tailored toward the particular needs of college students?

- What is the history of our program: how did we get to where we are today?

- What signals do students get through formal and informal channels about what matters in their undergraduate training?

o What special angle or perspective do we bring—because of our particular history, traditions, and culture—to the concept of integrated learning?

The process we envision here is not separate from the following proposed steps. Our intent in this first action item is to point to the need for a larger context of participation and deliberation in which particular steps are taken over time.

Review and reshape curriculum to support liberal learning goals for business students.

Though curriculum is not the only route to double helix integration (or a sufficient one), it is certainly its most important vehicle. The program of courses students are required to take sends signals and makes a mark like nothing else in their undergraduate experience. But we are aware, too, that curricular reform is a daunting task and an expensive one in terms of time, money, and sometimes, alas, peaceful coexistence among colleagues. How then to proceed?

For starters, questions about curriculum should be part of the process recommended previously. The questions that will need to be raised are big ones: What are our goals for student learning? How can they best be met? What will be taught, to whom, and by whom? In what sequence? And, very important, how do we know if our goals are being met? What processes do we (or should we) use to assess the quality and effectiveness of the education we provide for students?

As one way to engage these questions in a concrete way, we suggest a simple strategy that was useful in our campus site visits: when we talked with faculty about their courses, reviewed their syllabi, and observed classes, our observations were guided by a template asking about the presence of teaching for Analytical Thinking, Multiple Framing, the Reflective Exploration of Meaning, and Practical Reasoning and about whether the content and perspectives of the arts and sciences as well as business disciplines were included in the course. In our view, the goal should be a curriculum in which all of these features of liberal learning are encountered frequently by all undergraduates, including those majoring in business.

It may be helpful, as well, to realize that curricular change need not be an all-or-nothing undertaking. Some of the programs featured in this book are products of a broader and quite comprehensive curriculum reform effort on campus. Waiting for a curriculum review that will take place anyway is, of course, not necessary, but opportunities to build on those larger efforts provide added momentum and do tend to emerge frequently. In the absence of a major reworking of the curriculum, attention can profitably be paid to infusing courses in the existing curriculum with the various modes of liberal learning.

Additionally, curricular work can raise useful questions about what students do beyond the classroom; curriculum does not exist in a vacuum. It is important, then, to consider the institutional context in which coursework takes place and the contributions out-of-class experiences can make to students' development. A first step in this direction might be an audit of activities in which undergraduate business students participate.

Provide opportunities and resources to support faculty in their efforts to bring liberal learning and business education together.

Curricular reorganizations, especially those that create new hybrid programs and departments or new, integrative courses, raise the question of who will teach in those programs and where to find the instructional expertise needed for this kind of learning. Enrichment of existing courses raises this question as well. Given the disciplinary focus and specialization of faculty and the many demands on their time, integrative programs will not find this challenge easy to meet. Faculty development initiatives connected directly with the new or enriched curricula are, therefore, essential elements in the program's success. These initiatives help tenured and tenure-track faculty connect with the new approach, and they also help prepare the many nontenure-track instructors who may be hired to staff expanded or specialized programs.

If faculty development initiatives bring together faculty from arts and sciences and business disciplines, they can help bridge the commonly existing gulfs between the two and enhance communication. Centralized campus teaching centers can be a valuable resource in facilitating such interaction, be it through occasional brown bag lunch discussions, focused seminars, or more sustained programs of curricular and pedagogical improvement. Indeed, the notion of integrative learning in a broader sense has taken hold on many campuses in recent years (Association of American Colleges and Universities, 2007; Huber & Hutchings, 2005) and leaders of teaching centers may have special expertise to contribute.

Additionally, it may be useful to explore what kinds of faculty development opportunities are already available on campus and what is missing. Business programs often have special access to funding, for instance through corporate foundations, to support educational ventures of the kind described here. As suggested later in the chapter, joining forces with other campuses may open up additional possibilities and give heft and visibility to local efforts.

If they are well executed, faculty-development programs can be extremely valuable ways to stimulate greater attention to and communication about teaching. External experts can certainly make a contribution to such programs, but thoughtful, evidence-based conversation among colleagues is often the most powerful approach.

Develop a strategy to make liberal learning for business a hallmark of the program: explicit, visible, and fully intentional.

Liberal education has a long and noble tradition but it can also be a difficult concept to articulate. Abstractions abound, language means different things to different people, and misunderstandings can arise (for instance, the use of the word *liberal* may invite confusion with a political point of view). For these reasons, the vision of business education conveyed in this book brings with it a need to raise consciousness, to bring people on board, to develop, if you will, a communications strategy. This is an opportunity to educate about education.

Again, questions can guide action: Who needs to understand the double helix message? What other messages in the system might block effective communication of that vision? Where are the opportunities— many are needed—to convey an institutional commitment to liberal learning within business? We think, for instance, of program marketing materials, new student orientation, course syllabi, and communications from the dean and other administrative leaders.

It is not enough, of course, simply to *say* that a liberal education can be truly liberating or that it promotes a more satisfying career and a more fulfilling life. Rather, it is necessary to show why and how in ways that excite the interests and imaginations of students. Often the messages will be heard most clearly when they come from business leaders themselves—in honest, vivid, and textured accounts of their own experience, not in platitudes. Coordinated efforts in the curriculum, cocurriculum, and campus culture can reinforce those messages, especially when they also provide ongoing opportunities for students to practice them. In fact, students (and recent graduates) may be among the most powerful champions of the ideas in this book; look for ways to invite and showcase their voices.

Invest in research linked to educational quality and improvement.

Understanding how organizations learn and change is at the heart of business as a field, and this expertise can be productively turned on the efforts of the business program itself. As new approaches are tried—new courses, new classroom approaches, and the like—programs can make a commitment to couple innovation with evaluation, tracking and documenting impact in ways that colleagues can review and build on. To borrow a phrase from the field, business programs should be learning organizations when it comes to educational improvement.

The good news is that in many fields today, faculty (individually and collectively) are applying their scholarly habits of evidence gathering and analysis to the learning of their students. Engineering and medicine are notable in this regard. More broadly, what some are calling *the scholarship of teaching and learning* is bringing faculty together within and across disciplines to share what they are learning about the best ways to achieve their goals for students. (The Carnegie Foundation has been deeply involved in this movement.) By whatever name, we see this kind of work as integral to the previous items in this action agenda. Faculty development programs, for instance, are strongest when they include an element of inquiry—when they are undertaken as scholarly work rather than simply the learning of new techniques.

Further, research on the effects of educational improvement efforts can bring attention and prestige to the program and to individual (or groups of) faculty who take up such questions as a central part of their work. There are many opportunities today for sharing such work: journal articles, online resource collections, and face-to-face seminars and conferences. Going public in these ways is also key to giving teaching the recognition and reward accorded to other forms of faculty work. Senior faculty at institutions as distinguished as Stanford University and the University of Michigan have been granted tenure based in part on their research on education in their fields (Huber, 2004).

Partner with other programs, campuses, and organizations to create a collective voice and leverage for educational change.

In our earlier work on undergraduate civic education and on professional education in a number of fields, we have seen the power of institutional collaboration—among campuses and with national organizations—for strengthening educational practice. For instance, more than two hundred public universities have been working together for a number of years now to strengthen civic education on their campuses under the auspices of the American Democracy Project, which is cosponsored by the American Association of State Colleges and Universities and the *New York Times*. In the professional arena, we have seen a consortium of law schools form around shared efforts to update teaching and learning in legal education.

These collaborative efforts provide settings in which educators in the field can share insights and experience about what works, develop joint writing projects to disseminate their work more broadly, provide institutional legitimacy on participants' home campuses, and work together to generate resources for their reform efforts. We are not aware of national organizations with the specific mission of strengthening business education in the directions we advocate here. AACSB International, which clearly exercises significant influence over business education, has a mixed record in these matters. At one time, it accredited only those schools in which a majority of courses taken by undergraduate business majors were in the arts and sciences, but it dropped that requirement in 2003 when its mission took on a more international focus. Even so, the organization might be encouraged to support more integrative models with urging from leading business schools.

There are other possibilities for coming together to share efforts and develop a stronger collective voice for change. The Association of American Colleges and Universities (AAC&U) has been engaged for many years in promoting liberal education in ways that include vocational fields such as business. AAC&U is, therefore, an obvious body to support a national movement for the integration of liberal learning with business education. The American Association of State Colleges and Universities also has a long record of promoting collaboration among its member campuses in strengthening undergraduate education. It may well be a candidate for leadership in helping interested clusters of state colleges and universities implement the recommendations we have outlined. Smaller scale, perhaps regionally based, collaborations can also be helpful. We encourage business program leaders to find one another and forge relationships that can provide momentum and energy at home by sharing materials, faculty exchange programs, and campus visits.

○

Almost a century ago, Sinclair Lewis, the first American to receive the Nobel Prize in literature, gave a new name to those in business who are consummate conformists to society's mores. *Babbitt* became a household word that signified someone in business who takes no responsibility for society's organizations and institutions or its cultural values but simply and solely reflects the status quo. The novel is a biting satire and its protagonist a caricature, but Lewis effectively exposed troubling limitations in the business world.

Business schools today are now preparing their graduates to compete aggressively in the business world in ways that would have been alien to George F. Babbitt. But too often they fail to prepare those graduates to understand deeply what their lives could be about in any full sense or what their places should be in the world around them. As a result, they are not adequately prepared to be leaders in business or to gain full satisfaction in their personal and civic lives.

As the many examples in this book attest, this is changing. Surveying current challenges and opportunities, we have high confidence that the creativity, energy, and leadership within business schools today will create even more change, and that undergraduate business majors can look forward to a liberal learning experience that is preparation for life in all its dimensions. The growing importance of business in twenty-first-century life makes that goal more than a nice idea. It is a necessity for the individuals who enter business and for all who are affected by it.

REFERENCES

Ashraf, M. (2004). A critical look at the use of group projects as a pedagogical tool. *Journal of Education for Business, 79*(4), 213–216.

Association of American Colleges and Universities. (2005). Liberal education and America's promise. Retrieved from http://www.aacu.org/leap/

Association of American Colleges and Universities. (2007). *College learning for the new global century: A report from the national leadership council for liberal education and America's promise.* Washington, DC: Author.

Astin, A. W. (1985). Involvement: The cornerstone of excellence. *Change, 17*(4), 34–39.

Badaracco, J. L., Jr. (1992). Business ethics: Four spheres of executive responsibility. *California Management Review, 34*(3), 64–79.

Benner, P. E., Sutphen, M., Leonard, V., & Day, L. (2009). *Educating nurses: A call for radical transformation.* San Francisco: Jossey-Bass.

Bereiter, C., & Scardamalia, M. (1993). *Surpassing ourselves: An inquiry into the nature and implications of expertise.* Chicago: Open Court.

Bledstein, B. J. (1976). *The culture of professionalism: The middle class and the development of higher education in America.* New York: W. W. Norton.

The Board of Consultants. (1958). *The survey of the Wharton School* (report). Philadelphia: University of Pennsylvania.

Brint, S. G. (1994). *In an age of experts: The changing role of professionals in politics and public life.* Princeton, NJ: Princeton University Press.

Brown, T. (2009). *Change by design: How design thinking transforms organizations and inspires innovation.* New York: Harper Business.

Busenitz, L. W., West, G. P., III, Shepherd, D., Nelson, T., Chandler, G. N., & Zacharakis, A. (2003). Entrepreneurship research in emergence: Past trends and future directions. *Journal of Management, 29*(3), 285–308.

Campbell, B. M. (1995). *Brothers and sisters.* New York: Berkeley.

Chandler, A. D. (1977). *The visible hand: The managerial revolution in American business.* Cambridge, MA: Belknap Press.

Cheit, E. F. (1975). *The useful arts and the liberal tradition.* New York: McGraw-Hill.

Colby, A., Beaumont, E., Ehrlich, T., & Corngold, J. (2007). *Educating for democracy: Preparing undergraduates for responsible political engagement.* San Francisco: Jossey-Bass.

179

Colby, A., Ehrlich, T., Beaumont, E., & Stephens, J. (2003). *Educating citizens: Preparing America's undergraduates for lives of moral and civic responsibility*. San Francisco: Jossey-Bass.

Collins, C. J., Hanges, P. J., & Locke, E. A. (2004). The relationship of achievement motivation to entrepreneurial behavior: A meta-analysis. *Human Performance*, 17(1), 95–117.

Cooke, M., Irby, D. M., & O'Brien, B. C. (2010). *Educating physicians: A call for reform of medical school and residency*. San Francisco: Jossey-Bass.

DeAngelo, L., Hurtado, S., Pryor, J. H., Kelly, K. R., Santos, J. L., & Korn, W. S. (2009). *The American college teacher: National norms for the 2007–2008 HERI faculty survey*. Los Angeles: Higher Education Research Institute, UCLA.

Drucker, P. F. (1985). *Innovation and entrepreneurship: Practice and principles*. New York: Harper & Row.

Fisher, R., Ury, W., & Patton, B. (1997). *Getting to yes: Negotiating an agreement without giving in* (2nd ed.). London: Arrow Business Books.

Flexner, A. (1923). *A modern college and a modern school*. Garden City, NY: Doubleday, Page and Company.

Flexner, A. (1930). *Universities: American, English, German*. New York: Oxford University Press.

Foster, C. R., Dahill, L., Golemon, L., & Tolentino, B. W. (2006). *Educating clergy: Teaching practices and pastoral imagination*. San Francisco: Jossey-Bass.

Gaglio, C. M., & Katz, J. A. (2001). The psychological basis of opportunity identification: Entrepreneurial alertness. *Small Business Economics*, 16(2), 95–111.

Gardner, H. (1993). *Creating minds: An anatomy of creativity seen through the lives of Freud, Einstein, Picasso, Stravinsky, Eliot, Graham, and Gandhi*. New York: Basic Books.

Garvin, D. A. (2003, September-October). Making the case: Professional education for the world of practice. *Harvard Magazine*, 106, 56–65.

Gordon, R. A., & Howell, J. E. (1959). *Higher education for business*. New York: Columbia University Press.

Grossman, P., Hammerness, K., & McDonald, M. (2009). Redefining teaching, re-imagining teacher education. *Teachers and Teaching: Theory and Practice*, 15(2), 273–289.

Grossman, P., & McDonald, M. (2008). Back to the future: Directions for research in teaching and teacher education. *American Educational Research Journal*, 45(1), 184–205.

Gruber, H. E. (1981). *Darwin on man: A psychological study of scientific creativity* (2nd ed.). Chicago: University of Chicago Press.

Hart Research Associates. (2010). *Raising the bar: Employers' views on college learning in the wake of the economic downturn.* Washington, DC: Association of American Colleges and Universities.

Heckscher, C. C., & Adler, P. S. (2006). *The firm as a collaborative community: Reconstructing trust in the knowledge economy.* Oxford, UK: Oxford University Press.

Hendry, J. (2004). *Between enterprise and ethics: Business and management in a bimoral society.* Oxford, UK: Oxford University Press.

Hendry, J. (2006). Management education and the humanities: The challenge of post-bureaucracy. In P. Gagliardi & B. Czarniawska-Joerges (Eds.), *Management education and humanities* (pp. 21–44). Cheltenham, UK: Edward Elgar.

Higher Education Research Institute. (2009). *Commissioned analysis of HERI data on undergraduate business majors.* Unpublished report, Carnegie Foundation for the Advancement of Teaching.

Hovland, K. (2009). Global learning. What is it? Who is responsible for it? *Peer Review, 11*(4), 4–7.

Huber, M. T. (2004). *Balancing acts: The scholarship of teaching and learning in academic careers.* Washington, DC: American Association for Higher Education.

Huber, M. T., & Hutchings, P. (2005). *Integrative learning: Mapping the terrain.* Washington, DC: Association of American Colleges and Universities.

Hudson, L. (1966). *Contrary imaginations: A psychological study of the young student.* New York: Schocken Books.

Hutchins, R. M. (1955). *The great conversation: The substance of a liberal education.* Chicago: Encyclopædia Britannica.

Kanter, R. M. (1977). *Men and women of the corporation.* New York: Basic Books.

Katz, J. A. (2006). Education and training in entrepreneurship. In J. R. Baum, M. Frese, & R. A. Baron (Eds.), *The psychology of entrepreneurship* (pp. 209–236). Mahwah, NJ: Lawrence Erlbaum.

Kelley, T., & Littman, J. (2005). *The ten faces of innovation: IDEO's strategies for beating the devil's advocate & driving creativity throughout your organization.* New York: Currency/Doubleday.

Khurana, R. (2007). *From higher aims to hired hands: The social transformation of American business schools and the unfulfilled promise of management as a profession.* Princeton, NJ: Princeton University Press.

King, P. M., & Kitchener, K. S. (1994). *Developing reflective judgment: Understanding and promoting intellectual growth and critical thinking in adolescents and adults.* San Francisco: Jossey-Bass.

Kuh, G. D. (2008). *High-impact educational practices: What they are, who has access to them, and why they matter.* Washington, DC: Association of American Colleges and Universities.

Larson, M. S. (1977). *The rise of professionalism: A sociological analysis.* Berkeley: University of California Press.

Lauer, J. M., & Asher, J. W. (1988). *Composition research: Empirical designs.* New York: Oxford University Press.

Letcher, D. W., & Neves, J. S. (2010). Determinants of undergraduate business student satisfaction. *Research in Higher Education Journal, 6*(1), 1–26. Retrieved from www.aabri.com/manuscripts/09391.pdf

Lewin, R. (2009). Transforming the study abroad experience into a collective priority. *Peer Review, 11*(4), 8–11.

Light, R. J. (2001). *Making the most of college: Students speak their minds.* Cambridge, MA: Harvard University Press.

Martin, R. L. (2007). *The opposable mind: How successful leaders win through integrative thinking.* Boston: Harvard Business School Press.

Martin, R. L. (2009). *The design of business: Why design thinking is the next competitive advantage.* Boston: Harvard Business School Press.

McClelland, D. C. (1976). *The achievement motive.* New York: Irvington.

McDonald, L. G., & Robinson, P. (2009). *A colossal failure of common sense: The inside story of the collapse of Lehman Brothers.* New York: Crown Business.

Mizruchi, M. S. (2010). The American corporate elite and the historical roots of the financial crisis of 2008. *Research in the Sociology of Organizations, 30B,* 103–139.

National Academy of Engineering. (2004). *The engineer of 2020: Visions of engineering in the new century.* Washington, DC: National Academies Press.

National Center for Education Statistics. (2009). *Digest of education statistics 2008.* Washington, DC: Institute of Education Sciences.

National Research Council. (2000). *How people learn: Brain, mind, experience, and school* (Expanded edition). Washington DC: National Academies Press.

National Survey of Student Engagement. (2010). *Means and standard deviations by major: Senior students.* Retrieved from http://nsse.iub.edu/2010_Institutional_Report/pdf/2010%20SR%20Grand%20Means%20by%20Major.pdf

Nie, N. H., & Hillygus, D. S. (2001). Education and democratic citizenship. In D. Ravitch & J. P. Viteritti (Eds.), *Making good citizens: Education and civil society* (pp. 30–57). New Haven, CT: Yale University Press.

Nussbaum, M. C. (1997). *Cultivating humanity: A classical defense of reform in liberal education.* Cambridge, MA: Harvard University Press.

Orrill, R. (Ed.). (1997). *Education and democracy: Re-imagining liberal learning in America.* New York: College Entrance Examination Board.

Pascarella, E. T., & Terenzini, P. T. (2005). *How college affects students: A third decade of research* (Vol. 2). San Francisco: Jossey-Bass.

Pierson, F. C. (1959). *The education of American businessmen: A study of university-college programs in business administration.* New York: McGraw-Hill.

Rauch, A., & Frese, M. (2007). Let's put the person back into entrepreneurship research: A meta-analysis on the relationship between business owners' personality traits, business creation, and success. *European Journal of Work and Organizational Psychology, 16*(4), 353–385.

Rest, J. R. (1979). *Development in judging moral issues.* Minneapolis: University of Minnesota Press.

Santa Clara University. (2009). *2010/11 core curriculum guide.* Retrieved from http://www.scu.edu/provost/ugst/core2009/upload/Split-page-pdf-2010–11.pdf

Sass, S. A. (1982). *The pragmatic imagination: A history of the Wharton School, 1881–1981.* Philadelphia: University of Pennsylvania Press.

Schneider, C. G., & Shoenberg, R. (1998). *Contemporary understandings of liberal education.* Washington DC: Association of American Colleges and Universities.

Sheppard, S. D., Macatangay, K., Colby, A., & Sullivan, W. M. (2009). *Educating engineers: Designing for the future of the field.* San Francisco: Jossey-Bass.

Shulman, L. S. (1997). Professing the liberal arts. In R. Orrill (Ed.), *Education and democracy: Re-imagining liberal learning in America* (pp. 151–173). New York: College Entrance Examination Board.

Shulman, L. S. (2005). Signature pedagogies in the professions. *Daedalus, 134*(3), 52–59.

Smith, K. A., Sheppard, S. D., Johnson, D. W., & Johnson, R. T. (2005). Pedagogies of engagement: Classroom-based practices. *Journal of Engineering Education, 94*(1), 1–15.

Sorkin, A. R. (2009). *Too big to fail: The inside story of how Wall Street and Washington fought to save the financial system from crisis—and themselves.* New York: Viking.

Stern Business School. (2010). *Social impact core: Curriculum with a lasting impact.* Retrieved from http://www.stern.nyu.edu/UC/ProspectiveStudent/SocialImpact/SocialImpactCore/index.htm

Students in Free Enterprise. (2010). *About SIFE: Overview.* Retrieved from http://www.sife.org/aboutsife/Pages/Overview.aspx

Sullivan, W. M. (2005). *Work and integrity: The crisis and promise of professionalism in America* (2nd ed.). San Francisco: Jossey-Bass.

Sullivan, W. M., Colby, A., Wegner, J. W., Bond, L., & Shulman, L. S. (2007). *Educating lawyers: Preparation for the profession of law*. San Francisco: Jossey-Bass.

Sullivan, W. M., & Rosin, M. S. (2008). *A new agenda for higher education: Shaping a life of the mind for practice*. San Francisco: Jossey-Bass.

Trow, M. A. (1973). *Problems in the transition from elite to mass higher education*. Washington, DC: Carnegie Commission on Higher Education.

U.S. News & World Report. (2010). *Best colleges 2011: Best undergraduate business programs*. Retrieved from http://colleges.usnews.rankingsandreviews.com/best-colleges/spec-business

West, G. P., III. (2007). Collective cognition: When entrepreneurial teams, not individuals, make decisions. *Entrepreneurship Theory and Practice, 31*(1), 77–102.

Whitehead, A. N. (1967). *The aims of education and other essays*. New York: Macmillan.

Wiggins, G. P., & McTighe, J. (2005). *Understanding by design* (expanded 2nd ed.). Alexandria, VA: Association for Supervision and Curriculum Development.

Yergin, D., & Stanislaw, J. (1998). *The commanding heights: The battle for the world economy*. New York: Simon & Schuster.

INDEX